Dedication

To the men and women of the Hunger Project and the end of
starvation by 1997.

Winning Through Enlightenment

Ron Smothermon, M.D.

Context Publications
San Francisco

Acknowledgements

This book is a synthesis from many sources and is not meant to represent a particular source to the exclusion of all others. For the contribution of the idea of a Self, that when discovered, is whole, complete, and fully functional I acknowledge Karen Horney. For the contribution of the idea of a "space" in which relationships exist I acknowledge Harry Stack Sullivan. To Werner Erhard and *est* I acknowledge the general organization and language of the books. For the desire to contribute this material in living form I acknowledge the spirit of Judeo-Christian tradition. Finally, I acknowledge the person who made it all possible by making the word flesh: my mother. As my dear friend, she embodies grace and enlightenment so completely that she doesn't have a word for it.

Preface

Winning Through Enlightenment was written to challenge you deeply. It will challenge that unskillful part of your mind which denies "what is" in your life. It will challenge the many illusions that destroy your aliveness, your attempts to get your life to work by blaming others for the experiences you create, and the distortions that keep you stuck in feelings of separateness. It will also challenge that wonderful part of you that has the capacity to understand yourself and the world, to effectively change your life, and to love yourself and others increasingly. It can help you understand the roadblocks between your heart and the hearts of others.

Ron Smothermon does not spoon-feed you with long chapters of expanded explanation. He strikes like lightening—and then moves on. *Winning Through Enlightenment* contains enough "meat" for many books and will repay rereading many times. It is a book to be gradually absorbed. Many of its "secrets" for making your life work cannot be taught—they have to be "caught."

Winning Through Enlightenment offers you many rewards for effectively transplanting its life-giving insights from the printed page into the moment-to-moment operation of your mind. It does all that a book can do—it gives you the information that can transform your life. But only you, through your determined application, can develop the skills and insight that makes this knowledge effective in your life.

Ken Keyes, Jr.

Introduction

This is an introduction to a book, which is itself an introduction. It is an introduction to a way of thinking and living life that has been developing in the human potential movement for the past ten thousand years, perhaps longer. The material of this book is not intended as just another good idea. It isn't even about a system of approaching life that I believe in. This isn't another bandaid to put on your life, nor another "try this" approach. What this book is about isn't even what it appears to be about when you read the words. It is actually about you, but not the "you" that you ordinarily think of when you think of yourself. The "you" I want you to know about is the divine you, the one that includes, but is by no means limited to, the everyday "you." The purpose of this book is to present you with an opportunity to experience yourself as divine, a process that has been called enlightenment down through the ages. To experience yourself as divine, it is necessary to look at the everyday "you." Everyday you is described in Book I: Knowing the Mind. At times this may be tedious reading. You may feel insulted when confronted with the everyday you. Nevertheless, it is necessary to see all facets of the everyday you in order to see through everyday you to divine you. The terminology presented may be new to you. It will require some attention and some intention to make it through the following pages. It can also be wonderful fun. The result will be an expansion of your life and a commitment to participation you may not have imagined could be "you." I have written each chapter separately from all the rest, so that you may easily refresh yourself on the material as you lead your life. My sole purpose in writing these books is to serve you. I fully recognize the divine you as the true source of what you gain from reading this work.

All ideas written in this book are to be read and used at your own responsibility. These ideas are not meant to be a fail-proof recipe for how to live your life. You are responsible for what you believe in life and the consequences of your beliefs.

Table of Contents

BOOK I:
KNOWING THE MIND
(The Bad News)

This is a call to responsibility and enlightenment from the level of the abstractions which govern life as the abstraction of gravity governs falling. To get what you want from reading this, you will have to give up your resistance to your life working perfectly, wrap your personal life around these abstractions, and manifest your natural integrity. I can only remind you of that which you have always known and perhaps forgotten.

Chapter One:
Basic Mind Structure

The mind is an organ system that includes all of the physical being. The purpose of the mind is to survive and be right. To these ends it will do anything.

The mind is an organ system which includes all of the physical being. The purpose of the mind is to survive itself through the passage of time and to this end it will do almost anything. Sometimes, one thing ranks higher in importance within the mind, and that is to be right.

The mind accomplishes its purpose of surviving by laying down memory traces of events as they happen and calling upon these memories as needed in survival situations. Survival is involved in all functions of day to day life. There are memories, not only about what happened in the past, but also about what *could* have happened in the past to threaten survival. You don't need to have a memory about being run over by a truck to avoid being in the way of trucks. The mind can conceptualize what could have happened and then store the conceptualization as a memory. Man is man, the consummate survivor, out of this ability to conceptualize. No creature on the planet can conceptualize and store conceptualizations as efficiently as man. So the mind wires itself up very quickly to avoid those situations that threaten its survival.

The mind further accomplishes its purpose of surviving by seeking out those basic supplies it must have in order to avoid death. This is such an automated function that few people can tell you accurately exactly what is necessary for survival. Obviously air is required. Ordinarily the search for and use of air is so automatic that you are totally unconscious that it is going on constantly from birth to the present. An average of 18 breaths each minute total 9,460,800 inspirations and expirations each year alone. Almost as automatic is the search for and consumption of nutriments. Only when there is a shortage of air or food will the mind become fully conscious of its function of seeking out and consuming these basic supplies. The third and final survival need is not as obvious. However, without love from others you cannot physically survive. Death from love deprivation is most commonly seen in foundling homes where infants are given air and food but never touched in a loving way.

So, at the level of the mind, life is a game, the purpose of which is to survive. To successfully play this game people put together a survival act. Everyone has such an act. It consists of the behavior patterns which have the end result of obtaining adequate air, food, and love. Many false associations are built up over the years so that it is sometimes difficult to see that the way a person acts was originally related to survival. Nevertheless it all sprang from fulfillment of that purpose. Obviously, the way some people act does not promote their survival *now*; however, we often do not live now. Often we live *then* in place of now.

[You may have noticed that people have a certain need to be right. This is an aspect of survival. To state it correctly, being right represents successful survival ploys of the past. When they do not work in the present, what we see is a desperate effort to use them anyway because they are so strongly associated with what worked in the past. The truth usually is that being right and making others wrong does not promote survival in the present. Being right then is the one condition which the mind will sometimes choose over survival. *Sometimes* people will die in order to be right.]

Another important aspect of the mind is that it comes from a condition of insufficiency. What I mean is that the mind *says* that there is not enough of the basics of survival, so that what there is must be fought for. What this means is that within the context of insufficiency one person cannot gain unless another person loses. This context is the basis of competition. The competition, of course, is with other minds invested with the belief in insufficiency. Within the framework of competition rightness is given incredible survival value by the mind.

What is meant by "right" is nothing more or less than a judgement that the mind makes about itself, that its positions are right and the positions of others are wrong. The mind will use whatever circumstances it finds itself in to justify the conclusion that it is right. If the mind is of certain nationality, color, religious background, sexual preference, economic condition, political persuasion, or vocational choice, it will use that material to make itself right. The mind will use *anything* to be right.

Now, there is active rightness and passive rightness. Passive rightness involves taking *existing* circumstances to be right about. Active rightness means the *doing* of something to other people in order to be right. War is a gross example of active rightness. There are innumerable examples of less gross but active ways of being right in your own life. Arguments make good examples.

"Justification" is the process by which the mind takes the facts and interprets them in a way that suits its need to be right. Justification can do anything, including change your perception of reality. Even murder can be justified by the mind.

So the mind is a magnificent sophisticated machine which has required millions of years to evolve. It has the capacity to protect and reproduce itself, but its most remarkable attribute is its capacity to remember. It lays down a sequential linear order of all the events which happen within the sphere of its senses from the moment of conception. Although it doesn't have the capacity to call up these memory traces at will, under appropriate circumstances any of them can be reactivated. Some memory traces are not available to ordinary consciousness and are known as "unconscious."

This vast memory bank, most of which is unconscious at any given moment, accounts for a very interesting characteristic of the mind: automaticity. If you stop being a conscious observer of your mind, you will find that it survives quite well without you. It will do this automatically, without your participation, for that is its sole function. In order to survive, the mind develops patterns of behavior. When left unobserved these patterns run on automatic. In fact, patterning is such a strong quality of the mind that it usurps much of the experience of life itself and leaves one wondering, "Why am I doing this?" or "Why am I acting this way?"

Ordinarily patterns are of no particular concern to us. Our mind (includes body) machine simply does what promotes its survival. However, sometimes our behavior patterns cause us pain in our relationships. Some of our behavior patterns relate to relationships which we have had in the past. Around these nuclear relationships, behavior and feeling patterns are formed. The common feature of these relationships is that the mind has made an association between the characteristics of the relationships and survival. The primary survival needs associated with relationships are those of food and love. Therefore relationships that involve fulfillment of one or both of these survival needs are carefully recorded by the mind for the purpose of figuring out how to put together fulfilling relationships in the future, thus insuring survival. Your mind machine really works overtime on this one. The results are mind patterns based on what the mind thinks happened before, and these will then reach out to incorporate new relationships. Naturally, parents and loved ones form the nucleus around which survival patterns are formed. New people who come into your life tend to be viewed by the mind machine as essentially similar to your parents.

Now, no matter how fulfilling your relationship with your parents is or was, you are in big trouble if you become unconscious about whom you are with now. I promise you that the person you are with now is different and wants you to notice that. If you treat him or her with automaticity, you are in danger of losing the quality of the relationship if not the relationship itself. A mind does not have the capacity to experience or love others directly. It can merely record and react. A relationship, if it is to work, requires your participation. Your mind will not fill in for you successfully. It can only go through the mechanical motions of a relationship. The mind "needs" and you cannot love from the condition of need. *You cannot love who or what you need.*

So, to stay in the experience of loving a person, requires accurate and vigilant observation of the mind. Otherwise you become unconscious, treat others with automaticity and love dies for lack of your participation. This is the natural outcome of the unobserved (unconscious) mind patterns. Only you have the ability to observe. You cannot depend on your mind to do it for you since it is not in the scope of the mind's power to observe itself.

Chapter Two:
"Stuff"

*"Stuff" is the very substance of unreality. It is
your attachment to the illusions of life.*

"Stuff" is the term I like to use for all the content of the mind
that we carry around which we don't like, would rather not be
responsible for, yet which is undeniably part of the mind for
which we are responsible. It consists of all the beliefs, opinions,
positions, judgements, prejudice, all the mind structures which
serve the function of making others wrong and keeping us in a
condition of no responsibility.

There is no changing your stuff. It will change, very much as
a kaleidoscope image changes. However, there is no *willful*
changing of stuff. Moreover, you are not your stuff, although you
are responsible for it. What does that mean? Responsible for
what? It means that you are responsible for observing your stuff
and, although you can't change it, you are responsible for having
it and not mistaking it for the truth. This is called "transcending
your stuff."

Please don't make the mistake of thinking that you can
change the stuff in your life in any particular way. You can't.
Also, it isn't necessary to change any of it. For, you see, if you
know that it is just stuff, and not the truth, is not who you are,
then stuff becomes inconsequential. Really unimportant. Your
stuff is not important.

Not only is stuff unimportant, more than that, it isn't even real. Stuff is the substance of unreality. Carried to the extreme, stuff which is interpreted as reality is transformed into what is ordinarily referred to as "delusion." What is interesting about intense stuff is that everyone can see the unreality of it except the person responsible for the mind that invented it. At a less intense level a phenomen called "agreement" comes into play, which obscures the fact that the stuff you have is unreal. What this means is that other people share similar stuff in their minds and support your belief that your stuff is real. This creates a condition in which extraordinary integrity is required to transcend your stuff. In the process of transcending your stuff, you will go out of agreement with others and feel the loss of support. This tends to keep you stuck in your stuff. However, it is this very stuff which you are attached to which keeps life stuck in a condition of not working. NOTE

You may be asking yourself, "If my stuff isn't real, then what is real?" What is real has certain attributes. All that is real in this universe has a certain physical substance to it. That is, you can touch it, see it, weigh it, or detect it in some conventional real way. Another characteristic of what is real is that the mind tends to deny that reality when it comes into conflict with what the mind wants. The mind's favorite method of denying reality is to ignore it. How does this relate to stuff?

Stuff would not exist if what is real were noticed and given proper credit. You see, you don't need a judgement, belief, opinion, position, or prejudice for what is real. You need those things only for what is not real. The existence of life in this universe is real. You don't need to believe that life exists; you only have to check out your direct experience that there are living creatures around here. No belief in the matter is needed. You don't have to have an opinion that life exists or a position on the matter. In fact, if you developed a belief that life exists in this universe, your belief would make a terrific joke. Your stuff is a terrific joke because it is composed of belief, opinion, position, judgement, and prejudice about what doesn't exist. When you come to appreciate what a terrific joke your stuff is, then we say that you are enlightened. The way you feel about it is light. You know that it is not serious. You are on your way to winning through enlightenment. Others love to be with you, for you give them permission to be.

In the next few chapters we are going to go through stuff from several different angles. The purpose of this is to allow you to experience the fact that stuff is not serious. In other words, the purpose is for you to become able and willing to drop the extra baggage you carry through life that prevents the natural condition of joy in life. We want to make life available to you as it is instead of as it is not. We want you to become enlightened.

Chapter Three:
Judgements

The universal abstractions that run the universe were not created by the judgements of the mind. They just are and they don't care if you notice them or not.

To pass judgement is to create an artificial condition in which, by the definitions of your mind, someone or something is seen as better or worse than someone or something else. Therefore a judgement is a fabrication of the mind, the purpose of which is for the mind to make itself right. In the beginning, the purpose of being right is to survive. However, long after survival is no longer an issue the mind goes on passing judgements as if they were important in and of themselves. I want to remind you that there is this thing called truth (what is), and then there are the judgements of your mind (what's not). Judgements are never truth. If you are in the process of dealing with truth, judgements are not necessary. Judgements, you see, are substitutes for what is when you do not care to deal with what is.

If something is true it just is, and it doesn't even care if you notice or not. The universal laws that run the universe and life within it have not been placed into being by judgements of the mind. They just are, and when you are awake and attentive they present themselves to you and you notice them. You don't have to figure out. In fact, you can't figure them out. To get what I am telling you here, you must begin to appreciate the fact that you are not your mind. You *contain* a mind which is available for observation when you are willing to be conscious. You are infi-

11

nitely more than your mind. If you don't get this point you can
become stuck in the pride which is attached to your judgements;
you will develop a belief that you *are* your judgements and you
will not have observership of your mind and the judgements that
it contains.

Now, if you are still with me, let's go to the next higher
plane: there is no such thing as right or wrong. "Right" and
"wrong" are mythical creatures invented by the mind for the
purpose of being right. To have an experience of what we are
talking about here, I want you to place yourself in the general
vicinity of the nearest star. That star is approximately four light-
years away. From that distance you are peering in the direction
of the earth. Miraculously you actually spot the speck of dust
called the earth. Certain creatures have evolved on the planet and
they are up to some activities. Now, are those activities right and
wrong, or are they just activities? Obviously they are just activities. Only when you are close to them and feel threatened
(whether you are or not) do they begin to appear right and
wrong. Those activities you feel threatened by are "wrong" and
those activities that you are not threatened by are "right."

Although in ultimate reality there is no right or wrong, there
is definitely a condition called "consequence." You get the
consequences of the things you do in life. Until you wake up and
see that, you are truly lost. The consequences of being judgemental are loneliness and solitude if you are passively judgemental. On the other hand, if you are intrusively judgemental
the consequence is severe drama in your personal life. As you
can see, being judgemental doesn't work to produce satisfaction
either in your life or in the lives of others.

Don't make the mistake of trying to throw judgements out of
your life. Those that you have are ingrained and automatic,
"reflex" if you want to call it that. Trying to throw out your
judgements doesn't work. What to do about them is to be conscious of them and let them be. Gain observership on them by
being aware of them as mere judgements, not truth you have to
act on. Transcend your judgements by being responsible for
them. If you will let them be, they will let you be.

Chapter Four:
Belief Systems

*If what you believe is actually true, you don't
need to believe it.*

A belief system is a collection of sayings about a person, place, or thing which is designed to define that person, place, or thing so that it can be dealt with. Beliefs arise from your unwillingness to trust direct experience. Beliefs then structure your experience of the world so that similarities are emphasized and unique differences are not noticed. In fact, whatever comes by for direct experience that contradicts a belief system tends to be ignored or explained away as something unusual: "the exception that proves the rule."

It just so happens that belief systems create a false context called: "It can't be _____ ." It can't be done. He can't be real. It can't be that we could ever love each other. It can't be that I could ever succeed at school. My mother could never change. It can't be that my boss could ever be rational. It can't be that I could learn to swim. It can't be that anyone could ever run a four minute mile. It can't be that the world could ever be in a condition of no war and no starvation. It can't be that people can exist in close relationships without bitter arguments. Can it? I MEAN CAN IT? OF COURSE NOT! EVERYONE KNOWS THAT IT CAN'T BE!

Belief systems, then, limit what we are willing to experience in life and what we are willing to have happen in life. "Miracles" definitely do not happen within the false context of belief systems. Slavery was not ended within a belief system. It could only be ended from outside that belief system. Belief systems restrict and immobilize the way things are. Meaningful change happens despite belief systems, not because of them.

Your personal life is severely limited by your beliefs. You can never know the universe as it really is. You can only know your experience of it. Beliefs, then, shape your experience of the universe within narrow boundaries. Your world will behave in a way that will confirm your beliefs about it. People in your life will act in certain ways that will tend to confirm your beliefs about them. When someone does something outside your beliefs about him, you will simply find a way to include it within your beliefs about him *or* you will fail to notice what happened.

I know that you think that life works, when it does, because of your beliefs. I promise you it works, when it does, when you are out of your beliefs and into your direct experience. Life works *despite* your beliefs. Life is quite irrepressible, you see.

Now, I want you to know more about where beliefs come from. In the beginning of your life you had none. Neither did you have prejudice, opinion, position, nor judgement. Then someone you loved bribed and threatened you and made you a deal you almost couldn't refuse. The deal was to sell out the joy of your direct experience of life and adopt a belief about something. Beliefs are created in an atmosphere of fear. You feared the consequences if you didn't believe it. You would get sent to your room, denied supper, kept from the movies, spanked, sent to hell, not loved, and so forth, if you didn't believe it. The Boogie Man would get you, and back then, unlike now, that was serious. You didn't *have* to sell out, but you did. "They" only threatened you; *you* sold out. By the way, "they" are still only threatening.

I want you to know what you gave up when you sold out. You gave up your naturalness. You gave up your natural knowingness about life and became lost. You gave up your genius. Yes, you are a natural genius, except that your fear of going out of agreement with the world keeps you stuck in your beliefs, and that prevents you from expressing your natural genius. And *you* did it. No one did it to you. And you can reclaim it; no one can reclaim it for you. You can't read enough books, go to enough classes, get enough degrees, to reclaim it. None of that will reclaim it. Only you can. To do it you start with a willingness to consider the possibility that your beliefs are just beliefs and do not reflect truth. You begin by remembering what you always knew: the truth stands alone without need for propping up by your beliefs. The truth is not what you believe but what you experience directly.

Chapter Five:
Drama

*Drama is what you do when you have a dream
while you are awake.*

"Drama" is the intentional, although often involuntary, acting you do in life, which you believe is real. The purpose of drama is to prove to others and yourself how right you are. The condition you are in while you are doing your real life acting is called "victim." Being a victim justifies anything the mind cares to act out, no matter how destructive to yourself or others. In the extreme, suicide and murder are dramatic productions to prove to the world how right the actor or actress is and how wronged he or she has been.

Most people stop short of suicide or murder to prove how right they are. Most simply use drama in a way that murders the experience of life rather than the biological aspect of life. I call this process "murdering a relationship" when it involves another person and "stupidity" when it involves you alone.

As it turns out, drama is not a one time thing but endures as a mode of behavior in a relationship over long periods of time. The murder of a relationship is usually accomplished over a period of time rather than in one swift blow. Nevertheless, there usually occurs a time in a dramatized relationship when you actually *experience* your murder of the relationship and justify a giving-up process occurring. Usually drama doesn't end with the advent of the giving-up process. There still remains the issue of proving oneself right and justified in leaving the relationship. This requires more drama.

Another aspect to know about drama is that, although it is intentional, it is not conscious. To draw an analogy: if we had a programmed computer before us and pushed the right buttons to command it to do something that it had been programmed to do, and all circuits were functioning, it would do as commanded. It would have no awareness of what it was doing; it would simply do it. So it is with drama. When you are acting out your drama, you are a programmed machine with no awareness of your program. You are just doing it. There is an accompanying experience called "no choice." Since you are not aware of your program, there is no choice involved in whether or not you act out your dramatic program. You cannot stop yourself. It floods your consciousness that you are right and there is no choice about stopping until the drama is complete. This process may consume minutes or years depending on the nature of your program.

I call drama that requires years to act out "dramatic script." All dramatic scripts that require long periods of time are supported by day to day "soap opera." It is important to restate that this is an unconscious process that happens with only partial awareness at best and, as such, what you say about it is, "That's life."

There is nothing to do about what is unconscious in your life. By definition, it is beyond rational consideration. But how did it get there? It got there in the first place by lies. You see, when you tell a lie about life, the price you pay for it is that the part of your life that contradicts the lie goes unconscious. Therefore, what there is to do is tell the truth about that part of your life you *are* conscious about and not be concerned about what is unconscious. If you do that, then unconsciousness will take care of itself. The confrontation you will face as unconscious material wakes up is that your mind cannot stay "right." You can be certain that this will be a large confrontation, for the mind does not like to be wrong. So the barriers that your mind has constructed to make you right are the same ones that separate you from satisfying, nurturing relationships in your life. They are also the same barriers that keep you stuck with "reasons" why you are not getting what you want instead of actually having what you want.

Perhaps you are wondering exactly what I am referring to in *your* life. Only you can answer that question. I want you to know that the issues that have come up on the periphery of your awareness while you read this book, the ones you have shoved back, those are the issues that this refers to in your life. If nothing comes up, you are *very* unconscious. It's the stuff you are avoiding. It's that relationship you never quite completed, which you left hanging. It's that parent, that child you have never been satisfied with. It's that stuff you have attached to the thing you do or don't do for a living, that job which is torture for you. You know what applies. Now, in case you are beginning to feel guilty, read on, for I want you to know the true meaning of guilt in your life. Guilt is an essential part of your continuing drama.

Chapter Six:
Guilt

If you feel guilty, what that means is that you are going to do it again.

I want you to have perfect clarity about the meaning and function of guilt in your life. Therefore I am going to tell you outright what it is and then what function it serves. Guilt is a "feeling" which supports a "position" called "I am bad." "I am bad" is a position the mind chooses to have in order to gain acceptance (rightness) with itself and others. Guilt is a currency which people use to pay for the evil things they do, imagine they do, or simply imagine. Once whatever it is is paid for with adequate guilt, you are then ready to do it again. So guilt is a currency which is part of a mind-game designed to justify repetition of certain mind patterns despite a judgement that they are evil. Once again: guilt is the currency used to repay some real or imagined trespass so that the trespass can be repeated. Guilt therefore is an integral part of a cycle: trespass-guilt-trespass-guilt-trespass-guilt . . . and on and on forever. Guilt has absolutely no function in stopping something that is harmful. If you stop in a condition of guilt, it is despite the guilt, not because of it.

Clearly, guilt is not an honest "feeling" or emotion. Few emotions are honest, but guilt is totally dishonest because of the tendency to repetition that exists in the same pattern with guilt. To the world guilt says: "I won't do it again." To the mind guilt says: "Go ahead, you have paid your dues; now you can do it

19

again." Next time you feel guilty, take a look at what you are planning to do next. Better yet, take a look at what you *do* next, since what you are planning to do next may be unconscious.

So, in case you have been wondering what to do about guilty feelings, here it is: stop. Stop what? Stop feeling guilty. Do whatever you do minus the guilt. No one can spend the currency of guilt that you pay in any way that promotes a sense of aliveness. In fact, guilt can be cashed in on you by others and the cost is your aliveness. You can then use what they do to you to justify further repetition. Guilt clearly has no constructive uses, so be rid of it.

Let me warn you that when you drop guilt from your life and just do what you do and become responsible for it, something will happen. What will happen is that you will go out of agreement with others who are used to your guilt as part of their racket with you. You are going to feel strange out there all alone, different from the way you are supposed to be and different from the way you usually are. You will have the opportunity to restructure old relationships or terminate them entirely. People may even leave you. But if your relationship is grounded in guilt, you will be better off without that relationship.

What you will derive from dropping guilt is perfect clarity about what you want in life and what you want from other people. You may even find that you want to hurt others, that you have a hurt-others pattern. If that is the case, what you do about it is be bigger than it; you get to observe it and do nothing. Also, you will have the opportunity to be appropriate. If you do something that harms others, you will have the opportunity to really clean up your act instead of retreating to your room to feel guilty.

You can't face this issue of guilt in your life until you are willing to face the underlying condition. The basic foundation of guilt is the fear that you are the person you are afraid you are. You know the one. The one that is shy, inept, dislikes others, wishes them harm, has no courage, is stupid, and so on. Did you think you were unique in this? You aren't. To really deal decisively with guilt you must go to its core: the person you are afraid you are. The one you are trying to hold in check by feeling guilty. The one you don't want to be responsible for. If you are unwilling to confront that, you are sentenced to life imprisonment within your own mind. So, do yourself and the rest of us a large favor by confronting and being responsible for the smallness your mind is capable of. Only when you do this can you ever experience how big, how powerful, how truly beautiful your life naturally is. Underneath all that stuff you are afraid you are is who you really are. And let me tell you, whether you believe it or not, who you are is really magnificent. So much so that it puts all that stuff you are ordinarily proud of totally in the shade. The major characteristic of who is under all that stuff is someone who literally aches to make a contribution to life, someone who really wants it to matter that they lived. I want you to know that this is who you have been covering up with guilt.

Chapter Seven:
Jealousy

You can't really have what, or who, you are
not willing to not have.

Jealousy is the mirror image of guilt. Guilt is inner-directed and jealousy is outer-directed. It is the excessive concern in a relationship that the other person is not adequately committed to the relationship. The concern is accompanied by a panic-state associated with the thought of the other person leaving the relationship. Jealousy is a "feeling" and like all feelings supports a position that the mind has adopted. To deal with jealousy, then, we must focus on its origin: the idea or position that it supports within the mind.

It turns out that the position that it supports is *always* as follows: "I am incomplete and I require this particular person to complete me; incomplete people do not survive; therefore I must have this particular person to survive." Thus the person you are jealous of must stay and allow you to possess him or her or you have a fear that you will not survive in life.

Jealousy will create its own cause. By that I mean that it creates its polar opposite in the mind of the person you want to possess. The idea that develops in the mind of the other person is: "This person can't survive without me; therefore I must stay. But if I must stay, I cannot choose to stay." The mind will then develop a feeling to support this position which is called "entrapment."

If you and I are in a relationship and you give me no choice

22

as to whether or not you and I will continue in our relationship, then I am not in the relationship by choice. The condition of no-choice constricts my experience of you and constricts what is possible in our relationship. It can justify, in my mind, my feeling resentment toward you and my acting out my resentment in a number of ways. I *may* choose to act out my resentment in such a way as to truly support your jealousy. So jealousy works to bring about the condition it most fears: loss of the other person.

Jealousy drives others away so successfully because it is hostility with a mask. In this way it is a cousin to guilt. Guilt is hostility directed toward yourself, and jealousy is hostility directed toward another person. Both wear a mask in that the person who feels guilt or jealousy is the last to appreciate it as a hostility-equivalent. Nonetheless, the result is the same: damaged relationship.

To reiterate a bit: when there is no choice *not to be* in a relationship, then there is no choice *to be* in the relationship. This is a universal law: you can't really have what (or whom) you are not willing to not have. In other words, if you aren't complete without it, you aren't complete with it. You *will* lose what you are not willing to give up. In fact, you never really had it. Too bad.

What works to transform jealousy is to start telling the truth and stop lying about the matter. The truth is that you are complete right now, the way you are. You may be complete with an idea that you are not complete; however, that doesn't make you incomplete. You may have a feeling (desperation) to support the idea that you are not complete, and that doesn't make you incomplete either. You are complete *with* your ideas and feelings, *all* of them. So, you don't need a particular relationship. Notice that I didn't tell you that you don't need any relationship. If you have jealousy in your life, your condition is that you are stuck with the idea that you need a *particular* relationship. Of course you need relationship. Remember that love from another is essential to life itself. What you have to know is that you are responsible for creating the experience of being loved. You have to notice the relationships that *are* in your life and quit wasting your vital energy on those that are *not* in your life. Fortunately, there are many people in the world so that you don't have to rely on a particular person. Therefore, you can freely give permission to whomever you thought you had to have in a relationship to not be in the relationship. Again, if you have people in relationships by entrapment, you don't really have them.

Now a curious thing happens when you give people the choice to be in a relationship or not. All other things being equal, they will choose to be in the relationship. If other things are not equal and they leave you, so what? You never really had them anyway. Now you are free to have a relationship of choice instead of entrapment.

I want you to be very clear about this. Jealousy is something you must eliminate from your life if you want your life to be all that it can be. Be very clear about this too: you can't possibly love what you need.

If you happen to be on the receiving end of jealousy in a relationship, you have the opportunity to generate compassion for another human being who is going through some stuff in her or his life. What works is to not pass judgement and make another person wrong for the mind condition they happen to be in at a particular time. If you resist jealousy, what you will get will be more jealousy. This introduces our next chapter, which concerns the fact that you always get what you resist.

Chapter Eight:
Polarities of the Mind

Any position your mind takes creates its own opposition with mechanical reliability.

By "polarities" I mean opposites. Examples are north/south, up/down, right/left. These are natural polarities. We are interested here in unnatural polarities or what I call "polarities of definition." The mind loves to deal in polarities of definition. A polarity of definition is an invention of the mind for the purpose of being right. To be right about something, the mind needs a subject to be right about and someone to be in the role of being wrong. Therefore, the mind picks a convenient person and a convenient issue and defines a polarity. This is accomplished by defining the sides of an issue, then determining one side to be right and the other side to be wrong. Of course the mind decides to advocate the "right" side.

The LAW OF POLARITIES then is as follows: any position that the mind takes involves the definition of a "wrong" side of the issue and thus calls into being its own opposition, or polar opposite. In nature there are natural polarities. Within the mind there are artificial polarities of definition. Artificial polarities do not allow for completion and mastery but provide only for a condition of being right.

Polarities are the stuff out of which prejudice, opinion, position, and judgement are made, and the process of polarization is the foundation of all evil. Polarization closes all avenues through which human beings can communicate. It closes all

avenues through which we can have compassion with and nurture each other. Polarization occurs at such an unconscious level
that the results it produces seem to be a natural condition in the
order of things. Whenever you make someone wrong, *for anything*, you create the "other side" which then seeks to make you
wrong. You are the source of your own persecution.

There *is* something to do about polarization: be conscious.
Notice when you polarize an issue. If you are conscious about it,
you can then be at choice about whether to continue in your folly
or not.

Of course there is the other side of the issue. What if you are
on the receiving end of the polarity process? Well, it takes two to
play the polarity game and you don't have to play. If you do play,
you are totally responsible for the results. Not partially responsible, but *totally* responsible, for without your participation there
would be no results. If you find yourself plugged into the polarity
process from the receiving end, you may choose to stop or continue. You can't stop until you notice that you are plugged in. So
be responsible and notice; then stop. If you are willing to notice
the polarity process before you participate in it, you need never
be in another argument. I mean *never*.

Notice that I have not told you to stop communicating. It all
has to do with where you are coming from. If you are coming
from the position that you are right and someone else is wrong,
you are in for a long painful process. Come from communication
and nurturance of the relationship. Of *course* communicate!
Have your say. Really express yourself. Completely. You can
even raise your voice and stamp your feet, and if you are coming
from communication and nurturance it will all work out. But if
you are coming from polarity, you can be sweet and gentle and
the situation will go from bad to worse fast. And you don't come
from communication and nurturance to prove how nice and
good and right you are. You do it because it works.

You see, if you are going to be a really effective human being
you must expand to create a context large enough to include *all*
positions about the issues with which you deal in life. If you
have to define others as wrong, you constrict the space in which
they exist a *little*, and you constrict the space in which you exist a
lot. Expand your life. *Include* the way other people are within the

realm of humanity. *Be inclusive, not exclusive.*

I want you to know the polar opposite of your life working perfectly. The polar opposite is: righteous judgement of others, polarization, and exclusivity. If you are in this pit you are not wrong, and I want you to know where you are and what the consequences are. And you are there because you chose your way into it.

Chapter Nine:
Trying

Life works perfectly, naturally, when you are
willing to let it. When you try, you are not letting it
be naturally perfect.

"Trying" is a mental condition created by the mind. Synonyms include "struggling" and "efforting." The characteristics of trying are: (1) a sense of frustration, (2) a sense of futility, (3) lack of purpose, (4) a condition of no satisfaction, and (5) no results. Despite this bleak outlook you are exhorted to "try hard" by those who are supposed to know best. Life *can* work with you in a condition of trying, but, as with belief, it works despite your trying, not because of it.

The purpose trying serves is to introduce the element of sacrifice into getting the job done in life. Why have sacrifice in your life? It makes you right, for one thing. You get to run a victim act on others and gather their sympathy if they will buy your racket. The payoff, then, is in relationship with others. Trying sets up a built-in excuse so that if you don't get the job done you can say, "Well, I tried, didn't I?" You then have a "reason" why you didn't get the result and this replaces getting the result.

Don't be in confusion about trying and doing. Despite what you may have been taught, the two are not naturally related. If you performed a task and "tried hard," the result would be the same if you did the task effortlessly. What really counts in life are the results. To achieve maximum results it is wise to drop all unnecessary baggage to get the job done. The condition of trying is unnecessary baggage and only weighs you down.

Having read this, you may be wondering what to do with it all. Here is what to do with it: *stop complaining*. Complaining is also extra baggage that weighs you down. Stop complaining, first to others and ultimately to yourself. If you choose to create a condition of sacrifice in your life, that is your privilege. However, I assure you that others are not really interested in your sacrifices, although they may appear interested sometimes.

Notice that I haven't once told you to stop what you are doing and do something else. I am simply advising you to delete trying from what you do. Who cares if you "try"? I promise you I don't. I'll take the results, thank you, not how much you are sacrificing to produce the results. Get your attention onto what counts and off what doesn't count. You see, it really is OK to get what you want in life without sacrificing. We won't even tell anybody that you didn't suffer to get it.

The fundamental truth you must experience in order to kick "trying" out of your life is that life works *naturally* when you are willing to let it. It may not work the way you had it planned, but it will work. Actually, you have to *do something* to mess it up. This is so whether you "believe" it or not. Really get this: solutions just make the material of which you construct more problems. You don't need to add more baggage by believing harder or trying more. What will work is to dump extra baggage so that your road through life will be enlightened and you can win naturally, as it was intended.

Chapter Ten:
Reasons

Reasons only help you sound reasonable. They have nothing to do with your getting what you want in life.

Reasons, synonymous with "rationalizations," are those ideas and thoughts we say to ourselves to explain the way things are when we are not willing to be responsible for the way things are. Reasons are not to be mistaken for true cause. True cause is true cause. Reasons are excuses. They help you sound "reasonable" and give you a false sense of security that you are right. Reasons, in the world of agreement, make you right and others wrong.

It is important for you to know about the material of which reasons are constructed. The material is called "nothing." Reasons have the *appearance* of being created out of something. However, when examined, they are merely created out of other reasons. The characteristic of reasons which distinguishes them from true cause is that they explain things only retrospectively. That is, they explain the past but not the future. True cause accurately predicts the future.

Now, let's look at some examples. If you think you are unhappy with your husband because of the way your father treated you when you were small, everything that follows the word "because" is a reason. It is the "stuff" which you will give in answer to the question "Why?". You are true cause in the matter of being unhappy with your husband. If you would prefer not to be responsible for your experience of your husband, you may assign your father or your husband to be the reason you are un-happy. If you feel depressed because your supervisor treats you meanly, everything that follows the word "because" is a reason. Factually, you create depression and you assign your boss to be the reason.

You see, when you know who you are, you are actually so large that there exists no cause outside of you. If you can get what I am saying here, I want you to know that your life is beginning to clear up totally. If you can't get it, come back next year. Perhaps you will be ready for responsibility by then. You see, you are so large that you not only caused the experience of whatever is in your life, you are so large that nothing in your experience of life lies outside of you. Even the reasons you made up to explain the way things are in your life lie within you. You not only caused your experience of your life to be what it is, you also caused the reasons which you imagine explain it all being the way it is.

There is an aspect of reasons that I want you to be aware of: reasons do not work. They do not allow you to experience satisfaction in your life. They only create bitterness and an excuse to make others wrong. Since reasons do not work I want you to give them up. I don't mean not have them. I do mean simply recognize them for what they are: beliefs that you made up. Your mother, father, sister, brother, husband, wife, girlfriend, boyfriend do not cause what you experience. YOU DO.

I am not accusing you of being bad if you have a lot of reasons in your life to replace what you said you wanted. I *am* telling you that having reasons doesn't work. Accusations are for things we are not certain of. I am *certain* that you cause your experience in life. I am also certain that you have figured out some reasons that you think caused your experience. A reason can be a string of "logical ideas" or a person. It can be circumstances or events as well. You name it, and someone has made it into a reason to be the cause of his or her experience. So if you were/are rich or poor, hot or cold, green or yellow, none of that is the true cause of your experience of life.

I am not telling you that you have not had conditions thrust upon you. You probably have. What I am telling you is that what you made out of them is *what you made out of them*. You are true cause; there is no other. If you are beginning to catch onto this, be careful not to wear it as a burden or a medal of honor. What you experience in life is not wrong, even if you are *never* satisfied. Nor is one way better than another, so don't be full of pride and arrogance if your experience of life is mostly happy. I simply want you to get with WHO does it, that is, who creates the experience of life for you. When you get with who does it, "reasons" begin to drop away and your life begins to return to its rightful owner: you. As long as reasons are the cause of your experience, your life doesn't belong to you. You gave it away in order to have excuses.

Chapter Eleven:
Justifications

You have to be as enormous as you are to let others be "right."

Justification is the blending together of reasons in an effort to make them appear to relate to each other in a logical manner. It is the process through which the mind attempts to establish its positions as the "right" ones and seeks to obtain agreement from others about the "rightness" of its "stuff."

That which is justified is not directly experienceable, else there would be no need to justify it. Only those things which are not so are held strongly by the mind as positions. Of course it is possible to take a truth and make a position of it. However, there is no need to defend such a position. Justification is truly superfluous in the case of what is true.

So you can always discern it when someone is defending (justifying) what is untrue: you will hear much-too-much noisy protest from that direction. Likewise, you can easily tell when someone is defending (justifying) what is true: the position is easily given up for the truth of the matter to stand on its own natural merits.

Now, it takes a big person to drop a position held about something that is not true. It requires a really capable individual to allow others to be "right." When you hear someone running his justifications about how he is right and you are wrong, you have to be as enormous as you are to let that be. The mind has a built-in reflex called "make those who disagree with your beliefs wrong." So here is what doesn't work: try to stop someone from running his justifications about how right his positions are. What this does is energize those positions.

Here is what does work: let justifications run down. They do not have a natural energy source and depend on resistance to continue. You may have noticed that someone in the process of telling you how right he is sounds somewhat like a recording. That is because what you are hearing *is* a recording. He is not creating freshly, moment by moment, what he is saying but merely repeating what he has heard, or practiced saying, before. This process tends to run down rather quickly if allowed to go unopposed. I know that it *appears* that people who are justifying their positions seem to have themselves invested in being right. However, I promise you that only their mind is plugged in. Let them be "right." What do you care who is "right"?

But what if you find yourself running justifications? What do you do then? Well, by the time you are conscious enough to notice that that is what you are doing, you are already at a condition of choice. You see, only when you don't know you are doing something are you unable to stop. If you choose to continue running your justifications, you will notice a shift in your experience of the process. It will no longer be serious. It will become light, even silly, in your experience. You may double over with laughter. But you can't get there until you notice that you are running a recording and not being yourself.

So here is what to do with your positions. First, become conscious that you have them. Then notice that you are holding them in place with justifications. Then become enlightened about them. Remember, if what you "believe" is true, you don't need to believe it. If what you believe is actually true, it will all turn out in the end, whether you waste your energy justifying it or not. If what you believe isn't true, it will all come to nothing anyway, no matter how much energy you spend justifying it. So relax, your positions are not relevant. Give them no credence. Rely on what can be directly experienced. Eventually, drop your positions and cease justifying them. All that is just extra baggage on your journey through life. Be enlightened. Life works better when you are not weighed down by positions you feel you must justify.

Chapter Twelve:
Intention

You always get exactly what you intend.

Intention is a phenomenon that happens outside of ordinary awareness, the purpose of which is to determine the course of your life events. One always gets what one intends, regardless of what the mind says about it. Intention is formulated at a level of awareness that transcends the mind. If you are out of touch with that level of awareness, the events that happen to you in life may come as a surprise. You may or may not like what happens to you in life, but either way you will experience it as a victim, and have no sense that you caused it, unless you are aware. If you are aware, on the other hand, you know that you cause the experience of everything that happens in your life. You have the choice to be satisfied and nurtured by the events in your life or victimized and embittered by them. Either way you got the experience you intended to get.

If you have a sense of what we are talking about here and yet you are not aware enough to know that you cause your own experience, you probably are interested in knowing how to "tune in." I am going to tell you outright so that you will know. You tune in by having a *willingness to experience* that you are, in fact, the source of your experience in life, *even* when it *appears* that someone else is doing it to you and you don't want what you are getting.

I want you to do an exercise, the purpose of which is to allow you to experience the fact that you are the source of your experience in life. Place an object before you. It doesn't matter what object. Any object, including this book, will do. Now, answer the following questions. What shape is this object? Is it pleasant for you to look at? How much is it worth? Would it make a good gift for someone? Now you have an experience of the object. Who created the experience? Did your mother do it? How about your father? Or perhaps your best friend? Maybe the object created an experience of itself and thrust it on you? Seems silly, doesn't it? Obviously you created the experience of the object. And yet, most of us troop through life not being responsible for our experience of it.

Notice that person you don't like. You know the one, the one you don't want to see or speak to anymore. Now, just who do you suppose created your experience of that person. Your mother? Your father? Your best friend? Most likely you think that the person you don't like created an experience of himself or herself and forced that experience on you. Seems silly, doesn't it? Of course you are the creator of those negative judgements. No one made you have them. No one could possibly make you have them. The question is not whether or not you are responsible for the creation of your experience in life. You are and that's it. The question is whether or not you will own and acknowledge your responsibility.

You see, you have all the information you need to have your life turn out perfectly, even in the judgements of your mind. All of the facts are available to you. If you are ignoring the facts in life, you are responsible for having it turn out the way it does. The method you use to have it happen the way it does is that you choose to ignore and be unconscious of the facts. Of course, you haven't *wanted* to ignore reality and you *have intended* it.

This brings up the issue of what you want in life, which you may have noticed is not the same as what you get, that is, intend, on every occasion. Wants come out of the mind, and the mind's primary concern is to survive and be right. So, what you want is designed by the mind to place you in a superior righteous position and enable you to survive better. Actually, you are going to survive. To the extent that you are willing to experience that, that you don't "need" a particular person or thing to make it, to that extent you can align your intention with what you want. We call this condition "satisfaction."

In the event that it is not possible, that is you are not willing, to experience survival as an accomplished feat, what you *intend* and what you *want* will definitely not be the same. In that case there is only one way for you to find out what you intend: wait and see. Whatever you get in the experience of your life, that is what you intended. This is a view of your intention by retrospection and tells you what your intention *was*, not what it *is*. NOTE

Don't become concerned about your unconscious. Your unconscious is not the source of your intention, and if you believe it is you can waste a lot of time playing a lot of worthless mind games. However, your unconsciousness *is* the obstacle between you and your seeing clearly what your intentions are. The unconscious dwells in the mind and is made up of all that information which contradicts the lies that your mind has told over the years. It is not available to you, so don't be concerned with it. Be concerned about what *is* available to you, that is, what is conscious. If you start telling the truth about that consistently, and being responsible for your experience of life, the unconscious will take care of itself by dissipating.

Notice that I am telling you to be responsible for your *experience* of life. I know that things happen in life, the actuality of which you do not cause. What you cause is your *experience* of what happens. You are responsible for what you make out of it. If you are in the midst of a difficult life situation, your job is to get value out of it, not another "reason" life didn't turn out for you. On the other hand, I want you to know that you don't have to get value from it. You can choose to get no value instead. The choice is yours. Simply be responsible for the choice you make. You *will* get what you intend.

Chapter Thirteen:
Perfection And Your Victim Story

Your basic nature is that of perfection.

I want to remind you of something you knew long ago, when you were a small child, and which you forgot: you are perfect. Take a look at the next small child you see and you can experience directly that people are perfect. You *are* perfect, even *you*. Now, this is as clear as anything there is. Just as clear is the fact that there are blocks to the experience and expression of that perfection, blocks which are called "beliefs that you are less than perfect." Remember that you don't have beliefs for what is true. What is true is directly experienceable and doesn't require believing. So, if you have a belief that you are not perfect, I have no trouble with that. In fact, I expect it. But where would such an absurd belief come from?

Someone you loved and who loved you told you about your supposed imperfections and *you believed it*. There was no problem with it until you began believing it. Then there was a problem. In order to dominate and manipulate whomever you were dependent upon in those early years, you sold out and went along to get along. Now you are paying the price for selling out way back then. I want to emphasize that *you* did it. No one did it to you, no matter how "reasonable" it seems to say so. You didn't have to develop negative beliefs about yourself. You did it in order to dominate someone. Now, if you say that someone did it to you, what you are doing is making an excuse for yourself and a reason that things can't change now. The truth works. Saying

38

that someone else is responsible for your negativity does not work; therefore it is not true. What I mean by the phrase "it doesn't work" is that saying that someone else is responsible for your negativity does nothing toward changing your negativity around so that you can be in the natural condition of satisfaction. Only being responsible for it yourself works. You can chant little positive sayings about yourself for the rest of your life, and if you are not willing to be responsible for it, nothing works. What you have, then, is a mass of negativity encased in a lot of little positive sayings. However, if you will chant the truth about yourself in the context of responsibility, then the lies you have buried in your mind will be forced up for examination. You will become very clear about your own magnificence, which transcends pride and shame.

Therefore, start at the true generating condition of poor self-esteem: stop blaming others. If you are willing to do that, what you do first is stop complaining to others. No one really wants to hear you run your victim story anyway. Run it on yourself as long as you have to, but keep it to yourself. If you will do this and experience that you are the source of your own life and always have been, I promise you it will all begin to clear for you *naturally*, without "trying." Keep saying you are a victim and it will never clear, no matter how good your "reasons" for thinking so are. Remember, it takes years to put together a victim act. It won't clear up instantly, the very first minute you begin to tell the truth. You may have a *lot* of "stuff" to process through. It may take a long time and involve several life changes. Be patient and keep telling the truth, and your life will take care of itself.

When I ask you not to run your victim act by complaining to others, I am not asking you to stop communicating. I am actually asking you to communicate more. By all means communicate. Share your experience of life with others, even those experiences you remember from the past. You might as well enjoy it and share it since there is nothing else to do with it. Develop an awareness about what is your victim story and what is your direct experience of life. Then, when you notice your mouth running your victim story, turn it off (shut up). Silence under these circumstances is really beautiful. Enjoy it. Be enlightened in your silence.

Be enlightened about your entire victim act. It really isn't serious that you have one. If it were serious we would send you to jail. Actually, everyone I know has one or at least had one. It was an interesting survival game to play while it lasted and now there is a new game up for you called "This is it." What I mean by "This is it" is that you will experience the natural joy of life much more often if you play your life as if it were the only one you have. This *is* it, you know.

Your basic nature is perfect. I don't mean almost perfect, I mean totally 100% perfect and your natural condition is one of joy. You don't have to chant a mantra to know that. In fact you don't have to do anything to know it except know it. Know also that that other stuff you made up over the years and carry now as such a burden is the way it isn't. So *get* it! You *are* perfect! Now! Whether you "believe" it or not.

Remember also that others are perfect *and* they too have blocks to the experience and expression of that perfection. Give yourself a break and treat them as the perfect beings they are so that they will have a chance to manifest their perfection to you. Be enlightened. Be responsible.

Chapter Fourteen:
Reality

What is, is. What isn't, isn't.

Reality is what is and is not what is not. It is complete unto itself and doesn't care if you notice it or not. Reality is the collection of unchanging laws which run the universe. Gravity is a reality. The printed page in front of you is reality. The relationships you have in your life right now are reality. These are all manifestations of the basic law that runs the universe: WHAT IS, IS; WHAT ISN'T, ISN'T.

Unreality is what is not. It seems to care if you notice or not. Unreality is the collection of mind stuff which is subject to change at any time. Wishing things were different is unreality. The book you are not reading right now is unreality. The relationships you do not have in your life right now are unreality.

Now, although reality doesn't care if you notice it or not, *you* had better care if you notice it or not. Not noticing reality means that your life is cruising directly toward not working, that is, being in a condition of no satisfaction. How many times have you dwelled on the relationships you don't have and ignored the ones you do have? How often have you wished for that job you don't have and neglected the one you do have? When was the last time you wished you had different parents and didn't give consideration to the ones you do have? And what about living in another place? That would make life much better, wouldn't it? What about someone just coming along and saving you altogether? That would be nice, wouldn't it?

Well, here is a piece of news for you that is also immutable reality: <u>no one will ever save you</u>. Only when you notice reality and get into alignment with it will you experience being "saved." It is quite easy to cause success: just paddle downstream along with the river of the way it is, not upstream against the way it is. You will do this for yourself or no one will.

That is all I am going to say about reality as such. However, please notice that this entire book is about reality. "Reality" is just another name for truth. What this book is about is reality or truth. Truth is obvious only if you notice it and give it room to be. The mind is not equipped to do this since it is a right/wrong machine interested only in rightness and survival. If reality is to be noticed, you will have to do it since your mind can't. If you let your mind run the show, it will create a condition of unreality in order to be right. The price you will pay for your mind being right is lack of clarity about what is real in life. Someday you will notice that the price is too high, and you won't pay anymore.

Chapter Fifteen:
Illness And Disease

To prevent illness, inhabit your body.

Illness is a temporary disturbance in the sense of physical wellbeing produced by the mind in collaboration with external forces. The underlying disturbance of mind (remember that mind includes body) is called disease. Illness and disease have been generally assumed to be caused by external sources, and there has been little agreement that the individual can play a significant role in causation or termination of disease. These, supposedly, are truly things that happen to you, not that you cause to happen. Yet, everyone of us has experienced the rapid offset of illness when a more interesting game entered the picture. Children who are apparently sick become suddenly well when something enters the environment that they are truly interested in.

Of course there are influences in the world such as bacteria, viruses, and toxins. Yet some people are less susceptible to illness than others. From this fact alone we can deduce that the individual makes a significant contribution to the disease process. A high degree of consciousness and responsibility is necessary to go beyond belief systems about disease and we are now going to that level. *NOTE*

The truth is that when you are ill you are the cause of the illness. A bacteria, virus or toxin can serve to stimulate you, but the discomfort we call symptoms is your body's response to stimulation. If you made no response through your body, there would be no illness. All diseases are psychosomatic and all are expressed somatically. "Psychosomatic" is simply another way of saying mind/body or, as we say in this book, mind. You generate disease through your mind, even the most physical of diseases. The expression of the disease is through the body.

You mediate the course of illness through your mind. The mind accommodates by developing enormous belief systems surrounding illness. If you get a "cold," you are obligated by your beliefs to have it for three days. If it's "the flu," it should take a little longer and be a little more intense. Beliefs, positions, and opinions hold sway over the course of disease. Only to the degree that you can operate outside your belief systems can you deal directly with disease. Within the confines of the mind you are a victim, totally at effect, and it is done *to* you, not *by* you.

The mind cleverly uses disease and illness to dominate and manipulate others. Probably you are already semi-conscious of this fact. The advantages of disease in the area of relationship domination are immense. You can get out of being expected to be responsible for keeping your agreements in even routine activities. In addition to dominating others, you get to be right in many instances. Of course you are overworked, and you have sickness to prove it! Of course they shouldn't expect so much of you, poor thing! Perhaps you think I am referring only to how people manipulate disease. I am not. People *cause* their disease. Like much of the rest of life, however, this process goes on in a state of unconsciousness. "Stuff" is not just some interesting theory of mine. "Stuff" can make you very physically ill.

I can only remind you here of what you already know. You know when you cause disease and manipulate others with it. Even when you are unconscious about it, you know. All you have to do to know is know. Let's take this to the next higher level of awareness and responsibility. Chances are you will initiate a disease process that will eventually take you out. You are probably already doing this. If you are, you don't have to look far to see how you are doing it. Minor alterations in the way you eat, exercise, etc. have a profound long term impact on your health and you get to be responsible. All your "reasons" about why it is happening are just excuses for what you are really up to.

Since you are the being closest to your body, you get to be responsible for all that happens within your body. Be careful not to read this as blame or guilt. Disease is not wrong and you are not wrong if you have created disease in your body. Your body is your own and you may do with it as you like. And there are consequences.

Although there is nothing right about health, people tend to want to know how to achieve it. I won't bore you with factual information which you can look up. I want to tell you the ultimate truth about how to remain in a condition of wellbeing. Inhabit your body. That's it. It's not complicated. Inhabit your body. It is very difficult for disease to enter an inhabited body. Be here in this form until you are not. Be conscious. Be aware. Inhabit your body. You can't do anything more sanctified than to be where you are when you are there.

BOOK TWO:
ENLIGHTENMENT
(The Good News)

*A miracle is what happens when you are
going from one point to another in your life
and suddenly you are at your destination
without taking what you thought were the
necessary steps. These books are about miracles happening in your life. Life is a place
where miracles happen. To have a miracle
in your life, be alive.*

Chapter One:
Responsibility

*You are already responsible for your life, total-
ly. The only question is, "Will you acknowledge
that?"*

It is appropriate that this section on enlightenment begin
with a chapter about responsibility. True responsibility *is* enlightenment. False responsibility is endarkenment or enheavy-
ment. Everyone seems to think that they know the meaning of
the word "responsibility." In my experience, it, along with
"love," is the least understood among all words in the language.
Therefore, what you probably think it is, it isn't.

"Responsibility" is the willingness to be the author of all
your experiences, even the ones you don't like. If you create an
experience in your life which you view as pleasant or worthy,
you will be most willing to be responsible for it. You may even be
"proud" that you did it, which is a step away from responsibility. However, when you create an experience in your life which
you judge as bad or unpleasant, your mind will have the tendency to disown the authorship of the experience. Conditions or
someone else will then become responsible for what you have
experienced. Be aware that I am not referring to actual events that
happen in life, but rather to your *experience* of them.

So if you think bad things have happened to you in life, OK.
Now, I want you to know that is a position you have chosen to be
on. Furthermore, you are the agent who judged them as "bad."
There is no inherent truth in "bad experiences." They are an in-

vention of the mind to avoid responsibility. That should give you a clue as to what responsibility is not.

Responsibility is not feeling bad about it. Feelings are just supports for the positions your mind chooses to have in order to be right. So your mind will not only give you positions but "feelings" to support your positions, all in order to be right. So responsibility is not guilt or shame. If you feel guilt or shame, those are just feelings to support positions, and you are still a quantum leap away from responsibility. Responsibility is not a feeling. It is not a position. It is no more or less than being at source of your life instead of the victim of life.

Responsibility is not a feeling, but it makes appropriate feelings possible. Responsibility is not a position, but it makes appropriate positions possible. As long as you are stuck being a victim of life, you will force your mind to take inappropriate positions which bring along with them inappropriate feelings for support. Guilt, shame, and depression are examples of inappropriate feelings.

It should be becoming obvious to you that responsibility is where it is at. Just as obvious is that responsibility is the ground of being from which you come, no matter how far off course you may have strayed. What I mean is that you *are* responsible for your life no matter what you say about it. Where you want to be is in the actual experience of responsibility. To do that, you simply start to tell the truth about life. The truth is that you put it together the way you put it together. *And it is not bad. Nor is it good.* It just is. What you should get from this is that to be in the actual experience of responsibility you must operate outside the judgements of your mind. You can't do that until you unstick yourself from the idea that you *are* your mind.

By the way, being responsible does not mean keeping agreements. However, when you get into the experience of responsibility you will notice that all you can do is keep your agreements, effortlessly.

Chapter Two:
Enlightenment

Enlightenment is the natural condition of life after you strip the unnatural heavy and dark conditions away.

"Enlightenment;" much like "love" and "responsibility," is a much misunderstood word. So, I want you to be clear about it before we go any further. Many seem to think that enlightenment is a feeling, and it is not. Some think enlightenment is understanding, and that's not even close. There is nothing emotional or intellectual about enlightenment. You can't get it from your mother and you can't get it at school. It has something to do with love, but not as you probably understand that word.

There is a realm of experience that cannot be described in words. Any attempt necessarily falls short of the experience. Nevertheless, I am going to describe enlightenment in words since that is the form of communication available. However, we must know that words cannot be the source of enlightenment either. Words can only express the experience after the experience. They cannot generate the experience. Words do not generate enlightenment. Reading this will not make you enlightened.

Nor is enlightenment generated in the mind. The mind is only good for calculating how to survive. You will never experience enlightenment through your mind. The mind can only use words and "understand" enlightenment. I want you to really get frustrated about enlightenment and "try" to get it. You know what? You can't! It is just not possible for a person to generate enlightenment by effort.

You can only generate enlightenment by doing nothing. I mean *nothing*. By "nothing" I don't mean that you get a lemonade and go swing in a hammock. "Doing nothing" is possible while doing hard labor. In fact, it is easier to do nothing while doing hard labor. What I mean by "doing nothing" is to suspend your "stuff;" that is, your judgements, opinions, positions, beliefs, even your faith. Going through your stuff is doing something, *not* going through your stuff is doing nothing. Then do what you do in life because you are doing it, not because you believe in it, have a high opinion of it, or have faith in it. Doing what you do out of belief, opinion, or faith takes you out of the picture and makes your stuff the source of what you do. You land in a condition called no responsibility, no enlightenment.

What you do in life is not "heavy" until you add stuff to it. What you do in life is certainly not important from the standpoint of ultimate truth. *Not* important. If you think it is important, you are not the cause of it, your stuff is. Be light about your life. Live it moment to moment and in such a way that we could either ignore it or print it in tomorrow's newspaper, and it wouldn't matter.

You don't need to be proud or ashamed of your life. It just is. Nor do you need to be in control. If you are in pride, shame, or control, you are not the master of your life; pride, shame, or control is master. You can't be right, make others wrong, be proud and controlling *and* consider your condition important, and be enlightened.

Naturally, most of the description of enlightenment is a telling of what it is not. Enlightenment is the natural condition of life that has no name after all the unnatural conditions that have names are stripped away. I am now going to describe the condition of enlightenment for what it is rather than what it isn't. As I do, I want you to know that you conceivably could be in any or all of these circumstances and still be endarkened.

First of all, you will not experience needs beyond those that you naturally need: air, food, and love. You will know that your mind condition, whatever it is, is perfect even when you have judgements to the contrary. You will not depend on others to pronounce your life worthy. Criticism will be of no concern to you. You will not be criticizing others and you will not be attached to their criticism of you. You will be in the experience of loving others. You will know that life is not serious and that it *is* profoundly significant. You will know that others contribute to your life and you will acknowledge them for it. You will truly have what you own in life through a willingness to not have it and a willingness to share it with others. You will live in the present moment and not be attached to your memories of the past or your schemes for the future.

Chapter Three:
The Self

After you have named every "thing" which
you think might be you, what is left over, which you
can't name, is that which generated your life and all
that it contains.

Before I write anything about the Self, let me say that it can't
be done. By its very nature, the Self cannot be described. It is, in
fact, all that is not describable. Whatever you think it is you can
be sure of one thing: that is what it is not.

Nothing could be without the space to be in. I don't mean
"vacuum" which is just another mind concept "thing." We are
accustomed to taking for granted that there is a space in which
life exists. But think of it. Is it to be expected that there would be
this space? As you look at that, you realize that it is not reasonable to expect the space in which to exist to be. That space where
no thing is, which is continuous with all the rest of no thing
space in the universe in which you live, is the Self. It is the containing context for what we ordinarily think of as "life." What we
ordinarily think of as "life" is actually content. So Context or Self
contains content. The Self contains your life and is infinitely
larger than the content. Furthermore, Self doesn't exist in time. It
exists out of time and is the container in which time is contained.
Nor does Self exist in a place, or, said another way, Self exist in all
places and in no *particular* place.

The concept of a No Thing Thing boggles the mind, jams the
circuits. Add to that No Place and No Time and the mind is truly
at a loss to comprehend. You can't get this with your mind; you'll

have to get it with your Self. So the Self is that out of which life is generated, which has no aspect of thing, place, or time. Only a fool would attempt to describe such a what-ever-you-want-to-call-it in words. And yet words are what we have to communicate with, so here goes the fool.

Context contains what is. Context is not a what-is itself, however; otherwise it would be more of what is contained instead of the container. Context is the space which contains what is, *except* when we say it is a "space," it becomes a thing also and so the description breaks down. True Context is not a thing. You can't go somewhere and see it, and it exists in no time, past, present, or future. It doesn't even exist now, like everything else.

Context is the space in which the Self exists. Neither has any aspect of physicality, and yet Context Self allows all physicality to be. It is the unseen, unheard without which nothing could exist to be seen or heard. Context allows the physical universe to be. The Self allows life within the universe to be. This is accomplished by Context Self by not being.

I will remind you at this point that anything you can write or say in words is not it. Any concept your mind can have is not it. What can be said and conceptualized is simply more content which can, at best, point toward "it." Have you ever been with someone you loved and wanted to say something that could not be put into words? Well, that's it. What you *couldn't* say — that was it. Perhaps you did say something and then knew that, although it might have been beautiful, what you said was not "it." What you could not say, or even think — that was "it."

Chapter Four:
Context As Identity

You are the "other" universe which allows the
physical universe to be and constantly observes it.

What we are talking about here is giving the ultimate true answer to the question, "Who am I?" Much confusion exists around the issue of personal identity. Some of the untrue answers to the question follow; then we will proceed to the true answer.

People love to be identified. From the cradle you were given a name to bear through life for the purpose of identification. Most of us go through life thinking we are who the name we have says we are. Few people ever get so far as to question that. Almost everyone accepts her or his name as representative of who she or he is. Once that subtle issue is settled, it becomes easy to stack further definition over the name definition of who you are. Next comes sex, then skin color, race, religion, political party, possessions, place you live, social circumstances, opinions, judgements, and other "stuff." Now, I am not telling you that you don't have all that stuff in your life. You definitely do. What I am telling you is: that is not the ultimate answer to the question of who you are. The ultimate answer, by the way, is the one that provides satisfaction and workability to life. The interim answers merely serve to make you right and others wrong.

Go with me for a moment on a fantasy trip. Imagine a giant, clear plastic bag. In that bag let us place all of the things you think you might be. In first will go your physical being (your body), then your name, your color, race, religion, the place you live, your country of allegiance, all your clothes, your beliefs, opinions, and judgements, and so on until everything is included. This bag turns out to contain your mind as well, since that is a very crucial part of who you think you are.

Now, let us observe the bag. Are you observing it? If you forgot to include anything you think you are, go ahead and include it. Now observe it. Great! Now, who is that observing the totality of what you have called your life? That nameless, placeless, timeless observer is the one and only real true You. You are not the content of your life bag. You are the observer of it and you definitely contain all of that stuff. But that stuff is not you; it is merely within you. That thingless thing, that placeless place that exists in timeless time is Context. You are the Context of Life.

We now have a workable definition which will hold true on every occasion on which you want to know who you are. Nothing, I mean no *thing*, you define as you will endure and fit all situations. Context stands alone as the only true answer there is.

By now you may *understand* what I am talking about here, and that's swell. I want you to know that it will make no difference in your life until it penetrates the barrier of your mind so that you not only understand it but directly experience the truth of it. There is a part of every thing in you and a part of you in every thing. The absolute truth is that you are every thing, but obviously not in this universe. This won't make sense to your mind, which seeks its own separateness. So what? Who cares if your mind never gets it? What do you care what any of your content is up to? You have one responsibility in life: observe, observe, then observe. Contextualize your life in a way that works. You only real choice is contextualization. The content already is. What is, is.

Self, then, is Context. Contextualized Self is not available to ordinary consciousness. It can come into your awareness only when you are willing to let life be the way it is. Context is the placeless place where true choice is made. If where you make true choice in life is not available to your awareness — that is if you are a victim of life — then you have not been willing to let it be. Context is not the unconscious. The unconscious exists in the realm of the mind and is made up of all that information which contradicts the lies your mind has told over the years. Context is a quantum leap away from the unconscious.

Since you *are* the Context of Life, I advise you to *be* the Context of Life. I know this sounds somewhat vague *and* I know you know what it means. It all begins with an experience of your Self.

Chapter Five:
Acceptance

Life consists of cycles, that is, beginnings, middles, and ends. Acceptance allows a cycle to begin, commitment allows it to continue, and integrity allows it to come to its natural perfect end.

Don't presume that you know what "acceptance" means. Chances are you don't have the foggiest notion *and* you have a belief about what it is. Before I tell you what it is and isn't, I want you to know that it is the starting point of a satisfying experience of life. In fact, it is the *only* starting point to a satisfying experience of life. Obviously, something you cannot accept cannot be satisfying. In fact, if there is one aspect of your life that you will not accept, you cannot be fully satisfied with any of it. When you do not accept a circumstance of life, that means that you are not willing to acknowledge that you caused your experience of it. Even if it is only one aspect of your life, it will consume your energy, proving that your experience was forced upon you and the expenditure of this energy obscures the natural condition of satisfaction.

Now a word about what acceptance isn't. Acceptance is *not* sitting back and doing nothing about the way life is right now. In fact, what *you* may have difficulty accepting is not the circumstance of your life but what you are doing about that circumstance. Until you accept the way it is (which includes the way it is changing), you will have no choice in the matter. It will all go on in automatic. So, in the process of accepting life, you accept it as

59

it is; "as it is" usually includes the fact of change, so you get to accept it *all*. Acceptance is definitely not "doing nothing" in the ordinary sense of those words.

Acceptance is observation of life and suspension of judgements about whether what is happening in life is good or bad, right or wrong, *almost*. It *may* be that you will have to include in your observation of life the judgements your mind is making about it. You then accept your judgements of what is going on in the knowledge that your judgements don't mean anything. Thank your mind for sharing and go on. You don't need judgements for what is true; you only need judgements to make yourself right and others wrong. By now you must see that doesn't work. Ultimately then, acceptance is observation of life without doing anything differently. It is not what you do or don't do that reflects acceptance. It is the context in which you do what you do and don't do what you don't do that reflects acceptance.

It may *appear* that the most difficult part of acceptance for you is accepting the way other people are and aren't. I promise you, however, that isn't it. When you get underneath the condition of non-acceptance of others, what you find is non-acceptance of yourself. *Always!* I know you think you are an exception. You are not. Whatever you don't like in another person is always something you are afraid you have within you. In fact you probably *do* have it within you. That's just the way it is. While you resist it in yourself you will "not like" it in others.

So the external *form* acceptance takes is acceptance of others, and the actual *content*, what is real, is acceptance of yourself. So how will you know when you are there? The process of acceptance doesn't feel a certain way; however, there are certain signposts along the way. At first it will all seem the same. You will be disturbed about the way things are. Not only that, you will be disturbed that you are disturbed. Then you will notice that you are no longer disturbed about your disturbance. Next you notice that you are less disturbed about the way things are. Then you will notice that the way things are begins to look very OK with you, and you begin to notice that things have a purpose in being the way they are. Then you notice that you are the one creating the experience of how things are. Finally, you begin to participate in the way it is and contribute to it. You will be a part of it.

You may even *feel* a part of it. You will notice that your life matters and that what you do makes a difference. We just covered years of experience in a paragraph.

The people and things in your life may well remain exactly the same. Transformed Context doesn't mean changed content. It is your *experience* of it all that is altered. Your experience will be transformed in the process of acceptance. You see, you *really* are the source of your experience of life, and ultimately you are the source of your place in the world and the way people treat you.

Now, I want you to know why all this to-do about acceptance. Sometimes we feel stuck in life. And we are stuck. What we are stuck with is a memory of an event in life which we refused to accept and therefore could not experience. Because you refuse to experience an event, it becomes stuck for you. It becomes lodged in your mind and months or years later you are still stuck with it, that is, the memory of the event associated with an excessive discomfort. Acceptance allows you to have the experience so that you are up to date with your experience. When you are up to date with your experience, you are living right now. In other words, you are a full participant of what is going on in your life at the moment it is happening. When you are stuck on some past event, you will not be able to experience what is happening right now, and thus unexperienced memories form a backlog for you to deal with.

The body plays an interesting role in this process. The body armors itself with rigidity, positionality, and stereotyped movement to prevent you from having the experience of events stored in your memory. You end up with tension in your back, constant crossing and uncrossing of your legs and arms, headache, insomnia, and this sort of thing, which takes your attention off your actual experience of life. You experience your body instead.

The concept of time is also interesting in this regard. You will tend to become preoccupied with time, and checking and rechecking the clock to see what time it is. All of this, muscular tension and preoccupation with time, happens at an automatic, unconscious level.

To get through all of this defense your mind/body puts up, simply observe it and give it space to be. In other words, actually experience the events in your body in order to get past them. This goes for all the rest of your life as well. Acceptance is the key. You can't notice something or observe it until you have accepted it and let it be there to notice and observe.

Chapter Six:
Time

Time is an illusory construct of the mind to describe the fact that things change. Time is not real and things definitely change.

Time fascinates people on this planet like nothing else. Time seems to be as much a part of the human condition as the mind structures themselves. Time is conceptualized as a changing constant. It is never the same, and this provides the greatest intrigue of all. The mind personalizes time and spends great amounts of energy contemplating it. The life of the mind begins at a certain time and ends at a certain time. This is as sure as anything there is. Thus the mind makes time, the unreality, into something so ultimately real that thousands of "feelings" are generated to support the position that time is real. Grief at the loss of loved ones and anticipation of coming events are common examples of feelings that support the position that time is real.

Occasionally people become truly stuck in the illusion of time. Grief reactions stretch out for years, anger at events that happened long ago, even lifetimes of wishing life had turned out the way it didn't. As we have already seen, that which does not generate a condition of satisfaction is a lie by definition. Therefore, the idea that time is real is a lie, regardless of how real it seems to the mind.

Time, therefore, is a construct of the mind to describe the fact that things change. Time is no more than that. And things do change; in fact, that is all they do: change. The process of change is not something that the mind can alter; therefore it creates a description of it in an attempt to deal with it. Now, if time is not real, and change is, then the way life works is to be in a condition of noticing and giving space for change. The way it doesn't work — that is, isn't satisfying — is to try to stop change.

All the confusion clears up when we realize that there is only one "time" and that time is NOW. If you are willing to experience the truth that it is right now, your "problems" about the past and future will clear up. Why? Because there is no past or future; there is only right now. If you are stuck in what you call the "past," you are stuck right now. If you spend your time daydreaming about the "future," you do that process right now. You can't even go to these places called the "past" and the "future." *They are not real*.

If the past and the future are not real, what are they? The past is a linear sequential memory trace that exists within the mind, right now. You are aware of it only when your mind chooses to reactivate it. Your mind will choose to reactivate memory traces only to survive or be right and occasionally, for pleasure. So, the past is a memory trace. That's it. That's all. If you think you are sometimes troubled by past events, you aren't. You are troubled by a linear memory trace that your mind continues to reactivate in the present. Needless to say, the future is not. So, if you think you are troubled by the future, you can go play right field. Whatever you will ever bring into being in life you will bring into being in the present or not at all. This is another aspect of the "This is it" way of holding your life. Now is it. Nothing else counts. Nothing else is.

In the case of unexperienced life events, it becomes very real that now is the only time there is. As a person finally creates an experience to complete a past event, it "seems like" the event "just happened."

Actually, I am telling you that the only time there is is present time, or right now, for practical application. It works to consider there to be only the present. In reality, the present is not a graspable, testable thing, for as soon as you say it is the present, it is gone and there is no way to demonstrate that it ever was. It is gone in less than an instant; actually it is gone in no time. Even the present is not real. Time is not real. All is an illusion. Nevertheless, we are playing a game in which the illusion is considered real and what is real and enduring is considered an illusion. <u>Since this is what we are doing, let us do it with love and great energy. This is it!</u>

Chapter Seven:
The Body

The body exists, by nature, in a condition of wellbeing. It is a place to observe the world from. It is a physical representation of you, and it is not you.

The body stands as the most physical manifestation of Context there is. Contained in the human body is both the power to be and the power to observe being. The body has the unique capacity to shape itself by intention, unlike other physical manifestations of Context. In a very real way, body is Context. It contains the means to shape not only itself but all other forms of the physical side of Context. It actually thinks! Not only that, it thinks out loud. In the body is concentrated the collected intelligence of this corner of the universe from the creation of physicalness by Context. At an atomic level the body manifests the intelligence of being physical, the second most profound thought Context ever had. At the molecular level the body manifests the intelligence to arrange its atoms. At the cellular level the body manifests the intelligence of cooperation of Self, without which there would be no multicellular life. At the organ level the body manifests the intelligence of getting particular jobs done, such as vision, digestion, tasting. At the level of the individual the body manifests the intelligence of love and reproduction of itself. In cooperation with other bodies, the body manifests the intelligence of shaping the universe out of which it came. Context has actually developed a way to talk to itself.

Nothing determines physical satisfaction more than the context in which you hold your body. The body exists, by nature, in a condition of wellbeing. The natural condition can be obscured by inappropriate context. Let us discuss the context which allows for the experience of the natural condition of wellbeing.

The body is a physical place to observe the world from. It is a manifestation of you and it is not you. It is a form that you have taken. It is perfect and whole, regardless of what your mind thinks about it. It has the power to be and to observe being. It has this power because you gave this power to it. The body itself cannot observe. When you leave, your body reverts to simply being, without observation. The body is to be held in the context of what is. Not what is good or bad, simply what is. Look at the body from the standpoint of absolute reality. The purpose of the body is to be and observe being, not pass judgement on itself as good or bad. Do not buy the agreement system of the world which says some bodies are good, others not so good. It doesn't work; therefore it is a pack of lies.

Never use your body to be right. Jog, swim, eat the right foods, rest, and so on, because you respect your physical temple, not to be righter than someone.

Your body is marvelous beyond anything you can imagine. It is the physical representation of Context. It is a gift you gave yourself to enjoy and be. Always honor the purpose of your gift to your Self and forgive yourself when you don't.

Chapter Eight:
About God

*Either God is everything or there is no God. If
God is, God is. If God isn't, God isn't. Your beliefs do
not determine what is and isn't.*

I want you to know who God is and isn't, so that you will be
clear about it and not waste a lot of your life energy wishing,
hoping, speculating, and arguing. There are far more constructive ways to use your energy.

Man has developed powerful telescopes, visual and several
other varieties. For several centuries the universe has been under
close scrutiny and no one has seen a celestial person out there.
What this means is that if God is a celestial person, she lives at
extraordinary distances, too far away to be seen, *or* God is not a
celestial person. If God is a terrestrial person, she is quite well
hidden and, as yet, no one has located her earthly home.

Thus we know what God is not. God is not a particular celestial or terrestrial person. Who/what is God? What does God do
with her spare time? Does she really care? If God really exists,
why doesn't she speak up and end the confusion? Now I want to
become serious, or better said, I want us to become truly enlightened about God.

God is not what you thought God was. God is what God is. If
God is God, then she is all powerful. If she is all powerful then *all*
there is, is God. Otherwise there is no God. If one iota of power
or matter exists in the universe which is not God, then she is not
God and there is no God. *HM*

68

Obviously, the existence of God doesn't depend on what you believe about it. If God is, God is. If God isn't, God isn't. Who cares what you believe? So don't elevate your belief on the matter to the status of relevance.

God is the power in the universe to be and to observe being. That's it. God is the power in the universe to be and to observe being. All things and circumstances are generated out of this condition. Obviously there is being and observation of being; simple being and observation shows that by direct observation. Therefore God is. Or isn't. It's irrelevant, since what is, is, regardless of your position.

Obviously there are some concrete examples of being and observation of being around here. You are both. Don't get stuck in being proud about that. It is just what is.

But if you are a manifestation and embodiment of God, how can you be as you are? Well, you are and if you are interested in "how," tune into the way your mind functions. Evidently God isn't interested in placing relevance on "morality." It appears that God doesn't make "moral judgements" except through the mind. God is *the* power in the universe and included in the universe is "evil." If God is not the source of all things, then God is not God. So accept it! God is the source of evil. If God is not the source of all things, then God is not God. Therefore God is the source of all "evil" as well as all "good." To get this you will have to become unstuck from your mind which is stuck in judgements and polarities about "good" and "evil" motivated by survival.

The mind cannot observe. It can only be and *you* can observe it and record with it. An unobserved mind creates what we call "evil." The root of all evil is the mind's righteous condemnation of others and withholding your love from them. If you would like to clean up the "evil" in the world, simply be the observer of your mind and be responsible and be willing to acknowledge the scope of your own evil. When you are thus enlightened (responsible) the world begins to look more enlightened and responsible to you. In fact, the world is in the process of becoming conscious, responsible, and enlightened, and the experience of that is a gift I want to give you.

Chapter Nine:
Life After Death

If your mind dies tomorrow and life in the universe goes on, will there be life after death? How absurd can you be?

In place of the word "God" here, I want to substitute a couple of other words, which we have used before, to keep you unstuck from your childhood religious beliefs about God. I choose to use again the words "Context" and "Self" to represent the true God that is experienced by all, theist and atheist alike. You see, if our definition of God is so narrow as to allow some to have their experience of God legitimized and to deny others their legitimacy, we have done ourselves and the world a great disservice. Being right is a shallow substitute for having the world work.

Context then is that non-physicality that allows physicality to be. Self is that specialized Context that allows sentient life to be. No thing could be without the space to be in. If there were no room in this universe for your body, then your body would not be. Self, then, is a No Thing Thing, or a space, in which your physicalness is, without which your physicalness could not be. To the mind it seems natural that there should be a space in which its physicalness can be. But ask yourself why? Why should there be such a space? The truth is that space should not necessarily be or not be, and what we find is that it is. It is a gift from Context which we take for granted. It is an unconditional gift which demands no thing in return. In fact, within the spatial universe, vacuum occupies well over 99% of the available observable space. This place, in which things can choose to exist, is the profoundest thought Context ever had.

Self, then, is a No Thing, No Place, No Time thing, place, and time in which what you ordinarily think of as "you" exists, without which "you" could not exist. You can demonstrate all this to yourself in the physical universe by attempting to place two identical objects in the same place at the same time. Obviously they don't fit, therefore, this No Thing Thing has a non-physical, yet observable quality: "it" allows the presence of only one thing at a time. This is so obvious as to be taken for granted, that is, not experienced. Yet think of it; quit taking it for granted and experience it. As you do you will be in the experience of your real Self.

Our minds are accustomed to thinking of "life" as creatures, especially creatures that resemble our own physical form. Life, it is said, is intelligent, and so it is. Now go pick up a rock and hold it in your hand. I want you to know that the rock in your hand has great intelligence: it actually knows how to be a rock! Not only that, when "time" passes and it takes another form, it will demonstrate its knowingness about how to be that also. What that means is that right now the rock in your hand "knows" how to be that also. It is simply waiting until its time has come to demonstrate its intelligence. God, folks, is intelligent. God is a rock.

So God is all there is: both the space in which all things exist and all things as well. If there is one speck of dust, even one atom, in the universe which is not God, then there is no God. As you can perhaps see, this transcends "belief" totally and renders it obsolete. Belief is always obsolete when you rely on what you know.

Now that the framework is set, let's consider the question of life after death. From the standpoint of the mind/body there is no life after death except as it exists within belief systems. The mind does not care for the idea of non-existence, so it will construct belief systems to contradict the idea of non-existence. Nevertheless, what we are up to here is transcending belief systems and looking at what really is. Let me ask you a question so simple it is almost stupid in its profundity. If my individuality disappeared tomorrow, and yours lived on, would there be life after death? Obviously, there would be your life after my death. But what if I am not who I am supposed to think I am? Suppose who I really am is the Self. Suppose when I really know who I am, I am not my body or my mind or any of my individuality. Then can I not exist? I cannot not exist. I am. So are you.

In the interim when I know who I am, I am you. Ultimately when I know who I am, I am the universe and the space in which the universe is. We are God. This is the essence of enlightenment. And it isn't important; it just is.

HA HA The bad news for the mind is that it *is* who it is afraid it is.

BOOK THREE:
ABOUT YOUR LIFE WORKING

*You can't create beliefs that work in
life through the use of logic. When you use
logic, reasons always get in the way. You
can only create what works from nothing,
and you are responsible for the creation and
the consequences.*

Chapter One:
Agreements

Your life works exactly to the degree that you keep your agreements. An agreement has integrity because you make it, and for no other reason.

An agreement is a conscious pointing of intention. Now that you know about the Self I can tell you that intention is a manifestation of the Self. Of course you use your mind as the instrument through which you point your intention. In the case of an agreement, you agree to a certain goal. This involves the fulfillment of a commitment which you make with yourself or with another. The sanctity of an agreement does not depend upon the involvement of other people. The most profound agreements you make in life are those you make with yourself. An agreement has sanctity by virtue of the fact that you make it and for no other reason. The condition you come from in fulfilling an agreement is called integrity. Integrity is also a function of the Self.

The purpose of an agreement is to have life work, that is, to derive satisfaction from it and nurture life itself. Between you and your life working is the issue of keeping agreements with yourself and others. Between you and keeping agreements is the condition of the mind. The mind wants what it wants when it wants it and if an agreement gets in the way, the mind will go for breaking the agreement in order to get what it wants. Therefore, your integrity does not rest on the foundation of what your mind wants but on your willingness to keep agreements, no matter what excuses your mind dreams up to break them. The mind will go for immediate gratification at the expense of long term satisfaction. The only way to long term satisfaction in life is the keeping of agreements. Only through intention can you deal with your mind.

Never break an agreement! Never lie! Never cheat! Never steal! Not because these things are "wrong." "Wrong" is only a judgement and judgements don't work. Don't do these things because *they* do not work. You have a number of agreements that you have never said out loud or written down; lying, cheating, and stealing are among them. To keep agreements, you must first be in a condition of responsibility. You have to be responsible for the agreement. Ah! You say you didn't make the agreements. No one checked with you before those agreements were put on the books, did they? As a matter of fact you, as an individual, probably were not consulted. So what? Do you think we are interested in you at your smallest level? Sure, you can justify breaking the agreements if you want to be who you thought you were before taking responsibility for being enlightened. But I'll tell you, reality doesn't care about your justifications. The agreements are the agreements. Keep them and be responsible for them, and your life works. Don't keep them, and your life doesn't work. It's that simple. The source of the agreements is the Self. If you are willing to be responsible for being the Self and not just your mind, then you are the source of the agreements. Being the source of your life is bigger than you may have thought. It involves being the source of life, period. This is not a game you can play half-way. It's all or none. Choose.

What happens when you don't keep your agreements is that people get upset. The mechanics of your life do not work. You get to blame others. You have a reason life didn't turn out. An example is the issue of being on time. If you want to keep your life from really working, simply don't be where you say you will be when you say you will be there. I promise you, that will stop your life from being particularly satisfying. Also, you will lose friends and jobs. Keep your time and place agreements, and we begin to get the idea that your world is one that works. Everyone wants to participate with you if you are making your world work. It *is* your world, by the way. I mean *the* world is also *your* world. Until you accept that responsibility, *your* world *and the* world will never work. And I mean *you*, not the guy next to you.

Chapter Two:
Problems

*Problems are actually opportunities. The larger
the problem is, the larger the opportunity.*

I want to say a few words about a subject dear to the human heart. Without question people find themselves in circumstances and conditions which they did not create, which were created for them and thrust upon them. The fact that you have problems in life does not make you a victim, but handling your problems from the position of victim does. Some people have literally *born* themselves into circumstances so heavy with problems that it almost seems a cruel joke. For such people it is especially easy to allow circumstances to have the appearance of determining the presence or absence of satisfaction in life. It certainly *appears* that one has little or no choice in such conditions. So, set in the context that we all know that circumstances can be extremely difficult, I want you to know how to hold, or regard, such things as divorce, poverty, cruel parents, etc.

Problems have great potential for contributing satisfaction to life. In fact, the bigger the problem the greater its potential for contribution to your life. But *only* if you hold it as an opportunity. If there were no conditions to challenge you, there would be no real way for you to come to know about your Self and your capacity to make life work. If you had no naturally occurring problems in life, you would have to make some up in order to overcome them and thus experience your Self. You can be certain that people do exactly that. So problematic conditions are a tremendous opportunity to really have your life work and experience the workingness of it. Even more wonderful than that is that problems are an opportunity to really know yourself as your Self.

It just so happens that there are no circumstances capable of invalidating you. Only you are powerful enough in your life to invalidate you. If you do that, kindly take credit for it. If you think and feel that your life is not worth living, I want you to *know* that no one in your world could have been powerful enough to define it that way *and* make it stick for you, except you. Conditions and other people cannot do that to you. People have led worthwhile lives in the face of cruel parents, concentration camp, slavery, and mean bosses. Others have created joy and satisfaction in their lives in the face of mental retardation, no money, no education, no support from their parents, even no parents. I know that you think you are some sort of an exception, that your circumstances are special. No one ever had it as bad as you and, if they did, they certainly could not have had their lives work. Everybody knows that, right?

Of course you *are* unique. And no one ever had exactly your problems. Not exactly. But that is where it ends. You don't get to hide behind uniqueness even though you are unique and even though your exact problems are unique. You don't get to use uniqueness as a reason your life didn't turn out. If you don't handle your unique situations, it is that you don't handle them, not that they cannot be handled. The conditions of human life and the aspects of human experience are adequately similar from person to person so that it is evident that certain truths are always applicable. Maybe no one ever had problems with the father that you had problems with, but I promise you others have had big — I mean really big — problems with their fathers and handled it.

So much for the naturally occurring problems. Now, most of what you think are your naturally occurring problems are not naturally occurring. You actually made them up by clever manipulation and then disowned them and lied, even to yourself, about who authored the problems. People do this in order to have an opportunity to experience problems through. That is the purpose of problems. You will never know how capable you are until (1) you get off your victim position, and (2) use your problems as a way to experience yourself as your Self.

A "victim," as we use the word here, does not refer to a person who has problems, or even to a person who makes up problems without admitting it. A victim is a person who handles his problems from the position that (1) others have done it to him when they haven't, or (2) the problems are bigger than he is, or (3) he uses "problems" to justify something. In this sense all of us have been "victims" from time to time in life. But that game is getting called for the phony that it is. There are no "victims" in the sense that we are using the word here. There are people who source, or cause, their life content by using a victim act, but there are no "victims," not even you.

Once you get this, I want you to know that no one is powerful enough to make you handle your life responsibly. You don't have to, and you are not even wrong if you don't. And there are consequences. If you do choose to handle problems in your life responsibly, you won't even be right for doing it. And there will be consequences. There will be enjoyment and satisfaction in your life. You will have relationships that work. You will sleep well at night. You get to nurture others and be nurtured by them. You get to have the experience of loving others, making a contribution to life, and dying satisfied when that time comes. Notice the consequences of the context in which you hold problems; then choose what you want to be: victim or master.

Chapter Three:
Purpose In Life

At the foundation of every life is one central
desire: to make a difference that you lived.

At the foundation of every life there is one central desire: to matter. For it to matter that you have lived, for it to make a difference that you were here. This central desire to matter is called "purpose." Do not confuse this with the "reason" you are here. The reason you are here is something you have to make up and has to do with the specific content of your mind. It is the *form* your purpose takes, but it is not your purpose. By the way, *you must choose the form your purpose is to take. If you are waiting around for a message from God, forget it. You are the source of those messages.*

It is tempting to become more specific about forms that purpose can take, but that would be getting into the realm of mind stuff and that is not our purpose here. Judgements about what is good and bad are inevitable and ultimately untrue. So your judgements about what you do in life to manifest your purpose *are* present but are not important, even though you may have another judgement that says they are. Here we are not looking at content but rather at context.

When you strip away *all* the content, I mean even that content which you thought was context, down to the absolute basics where nothing further can be stripped away, something interesting appears. What appears is the fact that your life *does* matter, already, before you manifest "proof." It just does and that's it. You don't have to do anything to make it matter; it matters naturally. But human beings are peculiar, they like to see physical evidence that their lives matter.

There are perils on this journey toward manifesting physical proof that life matters. It is actually possible to obscure from your experience that life matters naturally. To do this you have to add something unnatural to life so that it begins to *look as though* it is different than it is. You have to put "stuff" on it. You have to take what you are doing and pass judgement on it. Perhaps you say that there is not enough money in what you do. Or you don't have enough freedom in your work. It could be the fact that people don't seem to notice your work that you will use to obscure your natural worth. On the other hand, perhaps you didn't get enough education. All of these things are judgements and, as such, are unnatural. If you take them seriously, in an unenlightened way, they form a justification system for obscuring the experience of your life mattering from yourself. You deny the nature of your being.

The natural condition, minus all the stuff to the contrary, is that of total perfect integrity, and that is what you have to deny in life to obscure your purpose. What you *do* to manifest integrity is keep your agreements. What integrity *is* is the willingness to let your true experience of life be what it is: true. Integrity is not putting something artificial over it. You can only experience that your life matters by operating at integrity. If you come from integrity, you will not have to be concerned about the form your life takes. All the form will take care of itself naturally without your having to worry about it or "trying" to make it happen.

What always happens when you come from a condition of integrity is that life is served, yours and others, and you experience the natural worth of your life. Your purpose becomes very real. When I say others are served I am not referring necessarily to exactly what you do. I am referring to the attitude in which you hold what you do. It is possible to serve others in the extreme and not experience your contribution. Actually, anything you do which is not destructive to others is a service. To have satisfaction about that, be willing to experience the contribution you make. Even if you are doing destructive things to yourself or others, if that is held in a context of contribution, it eventually transforms itself into a contribution. Even sweeping the street is a contribution, a very definite concrete contribution. You may never get credit for it except with your Self but, you see, it is only with your Self that anything matters anyway.

A sure way to obscure satisfaction in the form of your purpose in life is to get into the mind condition known as "pride." You can't come from pride and truly experience serving anybody, no matter what you do. I don't care if you are considered a very "important" person, if you are in a condition of pride, what you do will be of no service in your experience of it. For, you see, service is not a particular activity, it is the spirit or context in which activities are done. <u>The contribution is not what you do, it is the spirit in which you do it</u>. The perfect thing for you to do may well be right in front of you. What you have been looking for is not really something else, although you may have thought so. What you have really been looking for is your perfect *natural* context of contribution in which to do whatever you do. Only when you take responsibility for the natural context of it all will you actually experience the contribution that you make, that your life really does matter. Until then, no matter what you do, it will always seem to you that you should be doing something else.

Finally, I want you to know the deepest meaning of what you do when you do it in its natural context. It makes it possible for others to know that their lives really matter. It matters that we live.

Chapter Four:
Commitment

Commitment causes completion.

When you get the experience that life has natural purpose, and doesn't have to be manipulated in some particular way to be meaningful, you are then free to manipulate it consciously. The content of life that is most meaningful to deal with is that which relates to relationships. Commitment is the cornerstone of relationships. Without it there can be relating, but there can be no relationship.

Relationships exist within the framework of defined boundaries so that people know what they can and can not expect from you. Since commitments necessarily involve that which is relatively unchanging in life, and since the very nature of life is change, commitments should stick to the most fundamental components of life. What I mean by that is, as one of my clients once told me: "Keep it simple, stupid." Even keeping it simple, it is still up to you to define what those simplicities are for which people can count on you.

If people *assume* certain commitments in a relationship with you, you are responsible to communicate clearly enough that the assumptions are examined openly. Be clear that you can be in a relationship with the commitments, spoken and unspoken, or redefine the relationship, or avoid being in the relationship. Relationships in which you do not keep your commitments will not work for you. Hiding behind the apparency that you didn't know will not work either, and if you don't know, you are

responsible for communicating about it. You will probably discover that you do "know" about assumed commitments and you
would rather not acknowledge that you know.

Then there is the option of not making any commitments at
all. This is the formula for loneliness and works very well to
produce loneliness in your experience of life. People will avoid
you like the plague if they sense that you are not willing to have
commitment in your life.

To really make a commitment that you can keep, you must
have the experience that you don't have to make the commitment. If you have to, then you cannot choose to. If you cannot
choose to, then you cannot make a commitment. If you pretend
to make a commitment from the position that you have to, you
are merely setting up circumstances to justify breaking your
commitment. You get to have an excuse such as, "Well, she
didn't give me space to be myself." It was you who didn't give
yourself space, and you didn't give yourself space by your own
intention. To maintain a commitment in a relationship, you have
to experience that you don't have to make a commitment. Really,
you don't. Honestly, no one can make you. Absolutely no one.

Actually, a commitment is something you make with your
Self that sometimes takes the form of involving another person. If
you break a commitment you are ultimately untrue only to your
Self. They will get over it. You will never be the same. This also
goes for commitments that you make with your Self that do not
involve others, such as choice of vocation. It has to do with
completing the cycles of life. Acceptance is the starting point of
all the cycles of life. Commitment allows those cycles to continue
to completion. Until you complete any cycle you start, you are
never actually finished with it. The incompleteness of it will live
within you always. Commitment causes completion.

There is nothing mystical about this. You don't have to look
far for an example. If you have a bed not made in the face of a
commitment to yourself, there is an example. It's that cluttered
garage. That stack of dishes in the sink. That relationship you left
in mid-cycle. These things will live with you always until you
complete them. The nature of life is that it comes in cycles. So, if
you want a sense of completion in life, then the way to have it is
to keep your commitments. And you don't have to. No one can

make you do it. You can choose to be incomplete in your experiences. You are the only one who pays the price anyway. There is a time and a season for all things, so get in tune with the way it is. Have your life work. Complete your cycles. Keep your commitments.

Chapter Five:
Parents

As it turned out, you survived. Therefore your
parents did their job. Anything else you ever said
about it was in the service of being right.

"Parents" are those people who had a significant role in being with you and administering to your basic needs in early life, until you began to survive on your own without their assistance. Your biological parents may or may not have been your real parents. To deal with this issue of parents, you must correctly identify who your real parents were or are and give up your griping about those people who you think should have been your parents. It may be that you lived in the same household with your biological parents and had one or more additional real parents. Brothers, sisters, uncles, aunts, grandparents, friends of the family, and others serve us as parents. You may be unconscious about who your real parents are if you are stuck in a belief system about who your parents *should* be.

As with all relationships in life, the relationship with a parent has a purpose. Now, much is added to the real purpose of having a relationship with a parent. A parent is not designed to instantly gratify all of your wants and needs. Nor is a parent relationship designed to make you feel good about yourself. You are responsible for that. A parent is not designed to program you to make the right choices in life. You are responsible for all of your choices in life. The purpose of a parent is as follows: to be with you and assist you in surviving until you can survive on

NOTE

your own. Anything else you may have said about it, good or bad, has been in the service of putting yourself in a right position, so that you don't have to face the fact of your responsibility for your own life and the way it turns out. I mean this in both senses. It is fine and generous to give credit to a parent for your life turning out well, and it does not express the ultimate truth about it. It is absolutely evil to blame a parent if you feel that your life did not turn out. It is evil because of the damage it does to you: you sacrifice your aliveness. Your life will not work until you have acknowledged responsibility for it. Figuring out how your parents did it to you does not work.

Now, as it turned out, you survived. Therefore your parents did their job. No matter what you say about it, they did their job. Those people who had parents who did not do their job are not reading this, due to the fact that they did not survive. You, on the other hand, are living proof that your parents did their job. You know what? It isn't even your parent's job to have personalities that you like. Isn't that a kicker? I'll bet you anything you thought they were supposed to win some sort of personality contest with you. If you have baggage about any of this, unburden yourself. Life works better enlightened.

The issue of love comes up often with parents. The question frequently asked is, "Did my parents *really* love me?" What love is, is fulfillment of purpose in relationship, not that emotional garbage you thought it was. The truth is that if your parents put up with you until you could survive on your own (which they obviously did), then they loved you. That is, they fulfilled their purpose in your life. If you are not satisfied with the *way* in which they fulfilled their purpose, that is your problem, not your parent's. Don't you dare lay that one on them. You probably won't have any trouble noticing that you are carrying around a lot of "stuff" in life. It was no different with your parents. They burdened themselves with stuff too. In fact you were privileged to experience some of it. You probably liked some of it so much that you made some similar stuff of your very own. So when you become enlightened, by unloading your stuff, you do it by knowing that you are not your stuff and that you *are* responsible for it. We won't let you have double standards. If you are not your stuff, then your parents were not their stuff either. When you know that, you have an opportunity to relate to your Self for who you are, not who you aren't. Take and do likewise with your parents.

So the ground of being in relationship to parents is that parents and children love each other profoundly. And there are blocks to the experience and expression of that love on both sides. So what? It doesn't really matter if the form of the relationship never changes. Nevertheless people want the form of the relationship to change, so I'm going to tell you how to do it.

Let them be right. You be wrong. Who cares who is right and who is wrong anyway? Quit resisting them. Let them be right. You won't not survive if you let them be right. I promise you that what is under their need to be right is a deep love for you. By resisting their positions you block the experience and expression of their love for you, and your love for them as well. Where you want to be with your parents is complete on the past so you can begin to relate to each other in the present. You don't start on the road to completeness by being incomplete. *Being* incomplete doesn't exist. *Feeling* incomplete merely supports the position that you are right. Give up being right, and the experience of completeness, which has always been under the stuff, will be manifest in your experience. Make your relationship with your parents perfect, if you think you can handle it. You may have a need to be at odds with your parents. In fact, if you are, you do. So, if this is the case, what is up for you is to become aware and responsible for this kinky need so that you can give it up if you choose to.

By the way, your parents don't have to be alive for you to complete the relationship. Completion is a process of telling the truth that happens within you.

If you are willing to complete your relationship with your parents by telling the truth, it will then be possible for the rest of your relationships to be perfect as well. The thing about parents is crucial because that is the nucleus in which your mind patterns about relationships began. Until you clean that up, the whole thing is less than what is possible. As usual, you clean this one up by dropping the extra baggage of your mind stuff, thus being enlightened.

Chapter Six:
Children

Having children expands your experience of the world into the world.

The term "children" here means those people whom you have a commitment to assist in surviving until they are able to survive on their own. I am not necessarily referring to your blood relatives, or even to a particular age group. Parent/child relationships are generated spontaneously in life between people of all age groups as a manifestation of the Self's intent to be complete and satisfied. You may be unconscious about who the "children" are in your life.

It is important that a parent be clear about the fundamental purpose of being a parent, and that children share in the clarity of that purpose. The fundamental purpose of having a child is to assist the child to survive until such time as the child can survive on his own. If you have done this, you have done your job as a parent and you love your children. Remember that love is not a "feeling" but is the fulfillment of purpose in relationship.

While the purpose of the relationship is survival, certain other interesting things happen in the process of parenting. The one thing I want to focus on here has to do with your experience of the world. Remember that there is *the* world which you can never know, and then there is *your* world, the one of your perceptual experience, the only one you can possibly know, the one you put together the way it is. With that reminder you will be able to get this: your experience of the world will be expanded into the world through your children. That should give you a clue about when you are ready to be a parent. When your experience of the world is in a condition such that expanding it into the world will be a contribution to the world, then you are ready to have "children." I didn't say reproduce biologically, and that may be the way that you choose to have "children." Remember that "children" come in all sizes and ages, related to you by kinship or related to you just by being in relationship with you. Even if you are an adult with no offspring, you probably have children and you are probably somebody's child. So heads up; this applies to you too.

Having children requires something further. You must be in such a condition that you can actually assist another human being to survive. That, in turn, requires an *experience* on your part that survival is an accomplished fact. You can be rich as hell and still not have that experience. And you can be as poor as a church mouse and have that experience. So, it has little to do with money. Beyond the basic necessities of life, children are not nurtured by money; they are nurtured by parents.

It may be that at times you don't like your children. So what? Being a parent doesn't require that you like your children all the time. All children have unlikeable qualities. You may have noticed that children are manipulative. They are in possession of a mind which seeks to dominate and control others, just as your mind does. But where children are concerned, they are sometimes physically small, may not have much money, and probably have less power and fewer friends than you have. Therefore they will use what they *do* have to dominate and control. You may not like the way they do that, but they are sometimes plugged into survival just as you are. So children are not wrong for being manipulative. However, since you are bigger, stronger, richer, know more about the world, and have more friends, we will expect total domination of the situation by you, despite the efforts of your child. One way to dominate is to set it up so that everyone involved is satisfied and nurtured. In fact, satisfaction and nurturance are the most powerful instruments of domination available, for parenting or any other purpose. So express your power: satisfy and nurture your children.

Finally, I want you to know how your children will turn out

and how they won't turn out. They will turn out the way they turn out. They won't turn out exactly the way you had in mind. They never do. Too bad. Furthermore, they will do what they do in life, not necessarily what you advise them to do. They will make their own choices of life style, work habits, and sexual preference. You have no control over these things and you are not to blame for any of it. In fact, there is no blame for any of it when you operate outside the judgements of your mind. Your children are *individuals*. That means they are separate from you. They are not extensions of your own life. Make your own life satisfying for yourself and you will find that you don't need to live your children's lives. Ultimately, your only choice with your children is to bless them on their way or not to bless them on their way. I suggest that you bless them on their way as an expression of your love for them, even when their way does not line up with your judgements in the matter. Remember that they will do what they will do whether or not you bless them, so you might as well bless them in their lives. You can't make people be responsible. You can't even give them the choice. The choice is always there; you can only point it out. Remember that it is impossible to choose anything if you have to. In order to be sure that your children choose to be *not* responsible, try to force the "choice" on them. Lighten up with your kids! They are going to turn out. You may even turn out yourself.

Chapter Seven:
Sex

Sex is fun and pleasure is good for you, despite what you believe about it.

Sex is the aspect of body designed for reproduction. Man is a consummate survivor, and one way that this is expressed is the intense pleasure which has been built into activities causing reproduction of the body. Precisely because sex is so intensely pleasurable, the mind builds an incredible amount of stuff around sex. Of all of your stuff, conscious and unconscious, more than half of it relates to sex in some way. If your mind runs out of other stuff to think about related to survival of the individual organism in which you are dwelling at this time, most likely it will turn to that material which relates to survival of the species: sex. Sex is so ever present it has been repressed in order to get other jobs done in life. Nevertheless, relax for a moment and up it pops, so to speak.

Sex will be an active ingredient in all of your relationships whether you ever talk about it, or ever act on it, or ever think about it. You can like that, hate that, or be indifferent about it, and it will still be so. You will build mind structures around sex to contain and control it, whether you think that is necessary or not. You will learn when overt sex is considered appropriate within the agreement systems of the world, whether you agree with them or not. You will choose a sexual preference early in life which you will own for the rest of your life, whether you judge it good or bad. Obviously, sexual preference is not chosen by the mind, otherwise it would be amenable to manipulation. There is something mysterious about sex. Even after you learn everything that is factually known about it, there is still something you can't express. There is something about it for which there are no words. Even after you have taken all the communication courses there are, and all the sex classes available, there is still something deeply mysterious and inexpressible about sex. This is the base cause that people hesitate to talk about sex.

As you keep looking at that it becomes clearer that these aspects of sex resemble the aspects of Self. Both are essentially uncommunicable at the ultimate level. Yet because sex is so obviously physical, no one wants to look at the No Thingness of sex. Nevertheless, there is an aspect of sex that, like all experiences, occurs outside of the world of thingness, placeness, and timeness. Yet, at the everyday level sex is so mundane as to be like the plumbing of your house. It just won't all fit together the way we would like it to. It fits together the way it does, instead. Too bad.

Therefore, for sex to work, that is, yield satisfaction in your life and nurture others, you must see sex from all its facets, including the one which is called "no facet," that is, the part of sex which happens in experience (out of thing, place, and time). If you ignore one significant aspect of sex the whole thing won't work. You can't deny the truth and get results. The rest of this chapter will be about looking at the various truths about sex. As we do so, you may get nauseated, angry, righteously indignant, hopeless, or bored. I am telling you, you have a lot of stuff around sex. Accept it. Don't get stuck with trying to prove that you don't. You have a lot of stuff. So what?

The human body has a definite physical form. There are two standard varieties. One comes equipped with a long (sometimes) organ called a penis. The other variety comes equipped with a potential space in which to put the long (sometimes) organ. People who like to do this are called "heterosexual" or "straight." What they like to do is fill the space and create friction with their organs. However, prior to all of this there usually occurs an elaborate courting game with certain formulated (by the culture) behavior. Sometimes survival and love are rolled into the act and the whole thing is called "marriage." Sometimes survival alone is rolled into the act and it is called "prostitution." Sometimes love alone is rolled into the act and it is called an "affair." Occasionally this act produces new individuals. This may or may not be desired by the participants. Killing the individual before birth is called an "abortion." There are other people who like to relate sexually with individuals with the same body type as theirs. These people are known as "homosexuals" or "gay." Except for body configuration, and the substitution of certain orifices, the issues and the activities are exactly the same, except the creation of new individuals, and the issues that brings up do not apply. Sometimes sex doesn't work. The long (sometimes) organ won't become long or the space will not form lubrication. These conditions are called "impotence" and "frigidity," respectively. Some people are not able to make their organs work when they want to; others have their organs work when they don't want them to. During the sexual act, sometimes, people think about people other than the person they are with. Frequently people play with their organs for pleasure. Some people like to expose their organs; others like to watch them expose their organs. These two conditions are called "exhibitionism" and "voyeurism," respectively. Some people like to look at movies or pictures portraying sex or nudity. Others think animals are cute and are sexually aroused by that area. Some like to have more than one partner at a time. Still others prefer to fantasize about all or parts of this and never act on their fantasies. And some like to psychoanalyze it all.

I could go on, but I think you now have an experience that you have some stuff around sex. You think certain forms (almost always those forms that are different from yours) are "bad" or "wrong." You also have judgements that other forms (almost always yours) are "good" and "right."

Now for the real truth about sex. There is no right or wrong about it. Your belief systems are only belief systems, not truth. You remember truth. That's the guy who stands on his own merits, without support from your beliefs. More make-wrongs occur in the area of sexuality than any other area, except race.

Perhaps you remember that this book is about your life working? What that means in relationship to others, is being satisfied. Perhaps you also remember that it doesn't work to make others wrong? That it only makes you right and gives you a "reason" your relationship didn't turn out? Please get this: what is true in that statement about the rest of life is true in sex also. It doesn't work to make others wrong about their sexual form at the physical level. At the physical level, sex is just more mind anyway, and you know by now that people are not their mind stuff.

While it is true that there is no right or wrong in the area of sex, there are consequences. Sex gives us an enormous opportunity to exercise responsibility. It really is OK to have sex. Sex is fun and pleasure is good for you, despite what you believe about it. Be responsible while you are having all this fun and pleasure. Take the other person into account. Perceive what the other person makes of it. Perceive the possibility of creating a new individual. Have fun; enjoy your Self. If you want to use sex to *symbolize* the meaning in life, by all means, do so. Sex doesn't *give* life value; life is naturally valuable. However sex can make a nice symbol of the natural value in life. I advise you to keep survival and sex separated because it doesn't work too well to attach your survival to your sexual performance. Be really conscious when you associate love and sex. If this is what you want, be certain to pick someone who is into the same trip. If you aren't sure, ask. Communicate about sex. Say words that embarass you if the situation calls for that. Words are not "good" or "bad," "right" or "wrong" either, except in the unreal world of stuff.

The body is as clear a statement of Context as exists in the physical world. The sexual aspect of the body is as clear a statement of the Self as there is in the physical world. It is sort of a cosmic joke that it *appears* to consist of just so much plumbing. Sex can work for you at a level of satisfaction for which there are no words, if you treat it as a physical manifestation of Self. And sex can really not work at all, if you treat it as what it appears to be: just so much plumbing. There is a lot of baggage and a lot of stuff to unload about sex before it will work perfectly in your life. I suggest you start unloading and become enlightened.

Chapter Eight:
Money

*Money represents a false sense of security
about the probability of survival.*

Next to sex there is probably more stuff around money than
any other area of life. Money represents an enormous number of
unrelated issues. The complications that the stuff around money
can cause has driven some people and movements to avoid the
problems altogether by swearing it off as evil in and of itself.
Money is not the root of all evil. Even the love of money is not the
root of all evil. The root of all evil is man's intense drive to
survive, be right, make others wrong, dominate and manipulate.
Money just happens to be worked conveniently into this process.

Originally there was no "money." Money is an invention of
the mind to represent other physical property. The first monies
consisted of the goods that it came to represent later in history. It
was convenient if the money item was compact and easily trans-
ported. Examples of early money, still in use in parts of the
world, are eggs, clams, pelts, etc. Eventually, rough equations
were drawn up to represent the value ratios between various
items of money.

The mind of man is ever insecure and as far back as we know
anything about, people have been afraid they would not survive.
Sometimes this fear was, and is, justified, but more often than
not the facts support the probability of survival while the mind is
frantically considering non-survival. The experience of sure survival has been hard to come by in the history of man, and

therefore money came to represent a sort of false sense of security about the probability of survival. Out of this condition people came to covet money, and with this desire for money, power was placed in the hands of those with money in the hope of appeasing them and increasing chances of survival. If you look closely at all this, you can see that the assumptions are terribly absurd, even illogical. Never mind. People would rather feel safe than use good sense. Where money is concerned, people neither feel safe nor make good sense.

The mind creates a delusion that the Self is incomplete, that it is not whole and adequate. The mind further postulates that things will make it complete. Money represents things; therefore the mind goes for money in an effort to create an experience of completeness. However, the mind never acknowledges completeness. When it notices that there is still a sense of incompleteness, it goes for even more money. Sometimes the mind actually notices that money is not getting the job done. It may then conclude, irrationally, that money itself is the cause of this sense of incompleteness. Out of this stupidity people give their money away, only to notice that they still are not satisfied. You see, being satisfied and experiencing completeness have nothing to do with anything except being satisfied and complete. More money won't do it. Less money won't do it. Satisfaction is for a *very* select group of people: those who are willing to be satisfied. There aren't many around.

Your acquisition of money will not make you feel one iota more complete. But I am not telling you not to play the money game. In fact, if you live in this world, it is very difficult not to play it. I just want you to know what you can and cannot expect from it. Let's look at some attitudes about money that do not work. Then we will look at some that do.

It does not work to think of yourself as better than anyone else due to your wealth *or* your poverty. No one is served by this. It doesn't help you or others to be bitter about your financial condition. It doesn't help to develop belief systems about how "they" are doing it to you in the arena of money. All you will have is a pack of reasons rather than what you say you want. Looking to your parents to supply your money into your adult life doesn't work. Eventually you will have to figure it out. You might as well do it sooner than later. Looking at money as an end in itself doesn't work. Money is fairly cold. It will never love you and certainly will not keep you warm at night.

If you want money, go get it. There is plenty around and the techniques for obtaining it are thoroughly documented and available for you to read. There is no shortage of things in the world. If you want things and you don't have them, you must first experience your responsibility for your condition before you can clear it up. The rules for obtaining money legally are available for your study. If you think you want money, and you are not studying the rules, I conclude that you would rather gripe about not having money, than have it.

To understand money you must lighten yourself by dropping your belief systems about money. Until you are willing to get off your positions and consider the possibility that you might not be right in what you believe about money, money will continue to be a problem for you. Even with money, the way to truly win is through enlightenment.

By the way, money is easy to handle: spend less than you make and make more than you spend. You are not your money, therefore let *it* serve *you*, not you serve it.

Chapter Nine:
Perpetrations

A perpetration is a thought or act that denies another person her sense of aliveness. In the ordinary course of living we tend to justify, deny, or lie about our perpetrations. It could be said that this process is the source of all suffering in life.

A perpetration is the thought or act of something evil, criminal, or offensive about or toward another person. What we are most concerned with here is the doing or thinking of something evil, that is, something which decreases the sense of aliveness of another. I want you to be clear that a perpetration can be a thought as well as an act, and I want you to clearly understand the dynamics behind perpetrations, so that you will be conscious about your perpetrations on other people.

A perpetration is grounded in non-acceptance of the way a person is. This gives rise to the spontaneous thinking or doing of something to that person justified on the basis of the fact that the way she is does not go into agreement with your pictures of the way she should be. In other words, a perpetration begins *always* within you and in no other location regardless of the circumstances (which you caused by the way) and how well those circumstances appear to support your non-acceptance of the other person.

After you have justified your non-acceptance of the way another person is, you are very likely to do something, overtly or covertly, to decrease her sense of aliveness. You will necessarily have to go out of alignment with your Self to do it, and this results in an alienation from your Self. When this is complete you are free to provoke that person in such a way that she will act a certain way which will justify what you did to her as right and proper on your part. In other words, she begins to react to you in a way that supports the perpetration you have done to her and those you may choose to do to her in the future. If she doesn't react to your provocation, you will simply take whatever she does, alter your perception of it, and use your perception as justification for your evil. She begins to appear evil in your eyes and you begin to appear righteous to yourself. You may begin to tell others about her shortcomings. Your relationship doesn't work, but you have collected the reasons why not, and none of them relate to you.

The best way to handle perpetrations is not to think or do them, however, you may find yourself so unconsciously stuck in your perpetrations that you do not experience your choice to stop. *After* a perpetration your only choice that works is to communicate about it and take responsibility for it. If you do this, it will disappear from your experience, and the next phase, forgiveness, will appear, which will make your relationship whole and complete again.

Chapter Ten:
Forgiving

Forgiving someone is solid proof of your intent to live your life now, while you have it, and be dead later, when you are.

From time to time in life people will do things to you which definitely will not promote aliveness or satisfaction in your life. They may do these things over a period of years, with or without your cooperation. While it is true that you create the experience of having something "done" to you, it is also true that people *are* doing things to you. If you don't know that, you are in big trouble. I'll send you a road map to find your way home.

Now, while I don't want you to make people wrong for their actions, I definitely want you to hold them *accountable* for their actions. If you hold people accountable for their actions, chances are that things will never get to the point that you will have something done to you important enough to require "forgiving." If you don't hold people accountable for their actions, you are asking for it and you have probably noticed that you are getting it. What it means to hold someone accountable for their actions is that you *notice* their actions, then you *communicate* to them what you know about the consequences of those actions in this world. In other words, you assist people through their unconsciousness about what they are actually up to in their lives. That is what I am doing here, with you, by the way. To hold people accountable for their actions means operating outside the right/wrong system. When you make people right or wrong they become less conscious. In the case of making them right, they are not challenged to look at their life. If you make them wrong, they mobilize their defenses to ward off your attack and make themselves right. No one is less conscious than someone engaged in being right.

So, if you have been holding people accountable for their actions consistently, you probably don't have much to forgive anyone for. Probably you have been letting accountability slide and feel that you have a little or a lot to forgive. I want you to first be clear about what it means to "forgive," and then I want you to be clear about whom it is you are doing this forgiving for. What forgiving someone means is that you *give up forever all claim for revenge*. That's it. Period. Stop. Don't add any extra baggage to it. Keep it simple. To forgive means that you give up forever all claim for revenge. Notice that you don't have to give up *revenge*, only the *claim* for it. And get that word "forever." It carries the unconditional nature of forgiving. To "forgive" doesn't mean that you get to attach conditions to it. You don't even get to attach the condition called "I'll forgive you if you never do it again." Therefore, if they do it again you don't have to forgive them again; you already did that. Don't be repetitive. If you come to think that you have to forgive them again, you didn't do it in the first place. We will have to call what you did by some other name. So forgiving someone isn't a righteous ritual that you go through time after time. Hold it! I did not say that you do not hold them accountable. You had better hold them accountable unless you *really* want it done to you. What this means is that after you forgive someone for something, you are then outside the right/ wrong system. If they do it again, they are not wrong and they are responsible for the consequences. This should give you a clue as to *whom* you go through the forgiveness process for.

If you think you have forgiven people for *their* sake you don't know what it is to forgive, and you probably have never done it. Whom you do it for is *you*. They don't *need* to be forgiven. They did what they did and that is it — except for the consequences, which they get to live with. Your forgiving someone doesn't erase the consequences. The consequences are the consequences. So you are doing this "forgiving" for you, so that you can get off your grudge and get your life on the road. You see, you have a lot of vital life energy tied up in your grudges. By detaching yourself you get all that energy back. You can now make up even more mischief.

How will you know when you have forgiven someone? Well, you will know and you don't need a "how" for this one. It will be obvious to you, but oddly enough it doesn't "feel" any certain way every time. You may not feel any difference at all and chances are you will soon notice that you have more energy than you thought you had, but maybe not. One thing will definitely happen: your relationship with whomever it is will clear up remarkably. If it doesn't, then you didn't forgive. You will notice that you don't ruminate about how wronged you have been. You will notice that you sleep more soundly, perhaps, and perhaps not.

Forgiving is not complicated; it is simple. You simply identify the grudge and ask yourself, "Am I willing to waste my energy further on this matter?" If the answer is "no," then that's it. If the person is available you may want to tell them. But that is not what it is about. You are doing it for you, not for them. Therefore, telling them is just a little extra, added on at the end, if you want to add it. But to forgive, you really do have to get into a condition of honesty about what you are blaming whom for. Until you tell the absolute truth about it to your Self, you can't forgive.

After the truth is told you have to know that there is a choice: you don't *have* to forgive anybody. You can hang onto your grudges until you die and you can take them to the grave if you like. If you do, you are not wrong, for people choose to do this all the time. Bearing grudges to the grave is a style of acting in life. It would be out of style for some people to forgive, and what they should do is bear their grudges to the grave. So it *really* isn't wrong to blame and grudge, and there are consequences. Be certain that you see what the consequences are; then choose.

And I don't mean decide. I mean choose. Not for a list of "reasons" why you "should." You can't choose for reasons; that is called "deciding." When you choose something, you do it with clarity that you are the responsible agent. You *are* the responsible agent so you might as well have clarity about it. So choosing is not something we can make you do or not do. In fact, if you have to do it or not do it, you can't do either. *You can't forgive someone because you "should."*

By the way, if the person you have in mind is no longer living, that is of no consequence where forgiving is concerned. In fact, if they are no longer living that condition gives you a terrific opportunity to experience whom you are forgiving for. It certainly isn't them, and you surely don't have to forgive people.

Chapter Eleven:
Family

A family is something you create from nothing, not something that drops in your lap. If you don't bother to include people in your family, you won't have one.

Your family may not consist of those people you think it does. So, right now, let's get clear about who your family is and isn't. Your family is that group of people, perhaps only two persons, whom you trust and whose support you use to empower you to go forth into a world where there is adversity and actualize your purpose in life. A family in the sense we are using it here does not necessarily mean those people who are related to you by kinship. Those people are called "relatives." Your relatives may or may not be your family. There are no rules for this; you just look and see if, in your case, your family consists of relatives or non-relatives. If your family consists of non-relatives, then do not expect familial behavior from them. Depending on how you are manifesting the purpose of your life, your family may consist of two special people to thousands of special people who support you in manifesting your life's purpose.

Now, a family is something you create from nothing. It is not something that drops in your lap. If you do not bother to include people in your life, you will not have a family. If you have a built-in family of relatives, you will very quickly lose them as family if you do not bother to include them in your life as your family. Blood of kinship is not your guarantee of having a family.

You are responsible for creating a family, or not. Like the rest of life, it has to be created and recreated moment by moment. If it is not, it will become old, stale, and lose its meaning. So family is not something that you put together and then forget about. If you do, you will find yourself without one very soon. You must create your family every day.

Now that you are clear about that, let's go on to see the purpose of having a family. Why not not have one? Aren't they a source of hassle in life? Don't they account for most of your problems? Actually, they aren't, and they don't, but I want you to know that I know that they have the *appearance* of causing a lot of trouble. Some families are extremely good at creating this apparency. Of all the relationship structures that man has developed on the planet so far, family stands out as the one with the most "stuff" attached to it. This is a function of the mind's not wanting to be responsible for your experience of life. The mind will assign cause to every other place in the universe, mostly those places that are near. Family happens to be near, so family catches a lot of stuff. So, as we continue to look at it, it looks more and more as if you are not responsible, at least not totally responsible, for the way your family is. And that is true: you are not responsible for the way your family is, whether you judge it good or bad. Ah! But wait a minute. Remember there is *the* family which you can never know; then there is *your* family, the family of your *experience*, the only one you can ever know. There is *the* world and there is *your* world. You can only know about your world, the one of your experience. So it is with families also. So, are you responsible for your experience of your family? Well, if you aren't, to whom shall we look? Of course you are responsible for your experience of your family. If you did not exist, there would be no "your experience" of anything. So the purpose of having a family is to *experience* their support of you, to enable you to go forth and contribute to the enlightenment of a world in which there is adversity. You are responsible for creating that experience. If you have not, I don't care how "bad" your family appears to you in your judgements, you have not been responsible; that is, you do not acknowledge your responsibility for creating the family of your experience.

So family is sometimes a problem but remember that problems are an opportunity to experience your bigness. A family problem gives you the opportunity to experience what you are bigger than. You are fortunate to have one.

Chances are that, if you have problems with your family, you are focused on what you think your family owes you. I promise you that is not where the hook in the system is. The hook in the system is that you owe something to your family. And you had better pay, for your own well-being. You owe them your support. What I mean by support is not necessarily money. Whatever enables them to go forth and make a contribution to a world where there is adversity, that is what you owe them. If you don't pay, you won't have a family. If you are not experiencing their support, that is *not* a justification for not supporting them. In fact, you *cannot* experience their support until you support them. If you are wondering why you don't experience their contribution to your life, it should be becoming clear who is at the source of that. I'll give you a hint: it isn't them.

So what you want to do, *if* you want your family to fulfill its purpose, is to enlighten your experience of it. You do that by dropping judgements, opinions, positions, beliefs about them, and all that stuff that has them stuck in place being who they are not. Remember the steps to clearing up problems: accept them, be willing to be with them, drop judgements about them, be willing to be with them, accept them, drop judgements about them, be with them some more, accept them, drop judgements, and be with them. When you do this (which you don't *have* to, no one can make you), a miracle occurs. The miracle that occurs is that the family you have becomes the family you want, the one that nurtures and supports you, the one that truly empowers you. You will know when this process of enlightenment begins for communication will commence. Communication, then, is the subject of the next chapter.

Chapter Twelve:
Communication

True communication is generated in the "other" universe. The natural results of true communication are love and satisfaction.

"Communication" does not mean what you think it does. I am referring here to *real* communication. I am not referring to that mass of words and other motion that attempts to create the truth from what is not true. I *am* referring to that which reflects truth. The only way you can truly communicate is to tell the truth. To do that you have to transcend your mind structures, which are the source of untruth. What passes for communication in the world is a disguised form of lies cleverly made to look like the truth which is designed to dominate and manipulate others. Before you can go any further here, before you can begin to get a sense of what I am about to tell you, you must be willing to acknowledge that you are in confusion about true communication. If you were not in confusion and if you were really communicating, you would be running a joyous world. So I don't care who you are; what you call communication in your life is not true communication. Oh, it sounds good, and people tell you that it is good, but you must be willing to see that, no matter how good it sounds, it doesn't quite get the job done. If it did you would be running the world.

From time to time, however, you do have an experience of true communication. It happened at an unexpected moment, unplanned. It happened at a time, perhaps, when you did not

110

have your attention on communicating. It was that "magic moment" when you "fell in love." You remember it, and all subsequent efforts in the area of communication have been an effort to make it happen again. If you are really into it you have been reading books, amassing techniques, attending workshops, praying, burning incense to the gods, or whatever you do. All of this in an effort to bring "it" back.

I hope you have noticed that technique and ritual do not work. Only when you get into a condition of no hope about communication, as you think it should be, can you see what it really is. If you are not in a condition of no hope, I want to recommend that you go read some more books about communication technique, and attend some more workshops, or pray, or whatever you do. If you are convinced that adding more technique and ritual will clear up communication for you, do not read the rest of this chapter; you will just be more confused. You will be more confused because you will attempt to jam what I am saying into a "system" that you have learned. What I am going to tell you has no form, it is not a technique, and it will not work as a technique if you make it a technique.

Communication is not something you have to *make* happen. The only way it ever happens is when you *let* it happen. Communication is something that happens naturally. Efforting at communication only produces confusion and complications. True communication does not happen in the same universe with what we can see, hear, smell, taste, and touch. It has physical representation in this universe, but this is not where it happens.

I want you to get the idea of an experience. How long does it take to have an experience? I don't mean how long does it take to *express* an experience, I mean how long does it take to *have* an experience? You see, what you have been thinking of as an experience is actually the physical manifestation of the experience. Physical manifestations include tearing of the eyes, pounding of the heart, a light feeling in the body, and things like that. These are the physical manifestations of an experience but they are not the experience itself.

An experience happens in another dimension, another universe, so to speak. In this other dimension there is no time. So an experience happens in no time. I don't mean 0.0000000001 second. I mean 0.00000000000000000000 . . . to infinity second. That is absolute zero. Something that takes absolute zero to happen does not happen in this universe. It happens in the universe of all time and of no time. An event that happens in no time obviously doesn't have physical properties such as size, weight, color and so forth. If it did, it would exist in time. Something that does not have physicality obviously does not exist in a particular place.

What this has to do with communication is to introduce real communication. I mean *authentic* communication, not that fake stuff you get with technique. Real communication moves people and creates a condition of unity of being, love, and satisfaction. If what you call communication doesn't produce these qualities, then you have a technique, not the authentic article of communication.

The best we can do to express a no time, no thing, no place event is to say that it occurs in "Nothing." What could make this condition be? Obviously Nothing could make it be. What's more, Nothing has the capacity to allow everything be. Nothing is the source of true communication, and it takes the *form* of something. If you add up all of the somethings in the universe and consider them as a whole, what you see is that they exist as a whole, without reference points. There is no position of everything because there is nothing else for everything to be in relationship with. It doesn't exist in a particular time, since time is a function of change. When you consider everything, change is going on only relatively as a function of the internal workings of the system which involves the comparison of the *rate* of change. When you consider everything, there is nothing to compare it with so time becomes a fiction. Now let us reenter our universe of thing, place and time.

When we return to our universe what we see is that it doesn't operate very well at the level of communication when we fail to consider that Nothing generates everything. Nothing at the thing level is Context. At the human level we call it Self. Self is everything/Nothing with the capacity to communicate with itself.

Obviously there has to be more than one Self in the universe for communication to occur. If there were only one Self, communication would not only be unnecessary, it would not be. At the level of Nothing there *is* only one Self. At the level of *apparency*, that is, this universe, there are *many* Selves. The Context of the universe has evidently chosen to play a game by becoming individuals.

Now that the foundation, so to speak, has been laid for communication, we can now talk about communication. What it means to communicate is to generate an experience at the non-physical level, develop the intention to send the experience and have it received, then channel it into the physical realm and deliver the experience as a message via the body, which includes the voice, facial muscles, body tone, posture and movement. In other words, the Self delivers the experience through the machine. When the machine delivers a message on its own, no one hears or notices it, for there is no intention present. Intention to communicate is the essence of successful communication and comes from who you are. If you don't intend to communicate, your Self is not operating and your machine is playing mind games in your absence. No one notices except the other machines. This condition introduces a certain quality of automaticity into relationships and a substitute for communication which resembles a tape recorder. It tends to repeat over and over and over, the same stuff.

From the listener's position, receiving an experience involves taking it in through the physical realm and channeling it into the non-physical realm, that is, the Self. If it only goes into the physicality, it becomes a recording among many other recordings. If it is channeled to the Self it becomes a re-created experience. A re-created experience is an exact duplicate of the original experience of the sender. To tell the truth, it *is* the experience of the sender. Since there is only one Self at the non-physical realm, all experiences are not simply accurately reproduced, they are one. In this universe they are two.

So, to be communicative in the true sense of the word, there are two skills to develop: sending and receiving messages. I don't mean "develop" in the ordinary sense. Usually when you use that word you mean that you have to work at something to make it "better." I don't mean that. What I mean is that you drop the baggage of your mind so that what is already there can be manifest. The only blocks you have to perfect communication are your own mind structures. These include beliefs, opinions, positions, prejudice, etc. When you transcend these you will be amazed at what there is out there to communicate about. Dropping the baggage is called enlightenment.

Although this is the only chapter on communication, this whole volume is about your creating the conditions in your life so that total communication can occur. When this happens its natural byproducts will manifest themselves: love and satisfaction. This is accomplished by doing nothing. When you do nothing, communication is the usual, rather than the unusual, condition.

When you have totally communicated all the "bad" things and all the "good" things you can think of, and your mind is totally cleared of all that you have been withholding from others in your life, you will find that the bottom line is "I love you." That will manifest itself, perhaps even to your surprise and even in the condition of your belief to the contrary, after you have given up all the things you thought you couldn't or shouldn't communicate. To stay in the experience that you love someone, simply never withhold any communication.

Next we are going to look at the opposite of communication: arguments.

Chapter Thirteen:
Arguments

Arguing is what you do when you have no purpose, want to be right, are not willing to be responsible for your experience, and are bored. If you know that it is OK to argue, you are truly enlightened.

So we will be on the same wave-length, I will here define "argument." An argument is a verbal conflict of belief systems, the purpose of which is to make the other person wrong and put together the reasons why the relationship didn't work, in place of having a working relationship. If it doesn't fit this definition, it is not an argument and what I am about to say here doesn't apply. It just so happens that much unconsciousness is plastered over arguments so that it will be difficult for you to see if what you have are arguments or not. If you are not clear if what you have are arguments or not, they are. The revealing clue about it is your lack of clarity.

Now, there is a lie going around that arguments are inevitable. Many people are stuck in this lie and turn to making the best they can of a bad situation through making arguing "therapeutic." Nothing is wrong with this, and if you buy into the lie that arguments are inevitable, "therapeutic" arguing is what your relationships will be about.

Let me ask you a question. If you were in an argument and suddenly became the other person, what would happen to the argument? Would you continue to defend your positions, beliefs, and judgements and make the other person wrong?

Remember now that you have become the other person and you are still yourself. The argument would become obsolete, wouldn't it? So, let me tell you the ultimate truth about it: you *are* the other person. When you really know who you are, you are the other person. The "other person" is an extension of your own perceptions and, even beyond that, defying accurate description, you *are* the other person. Their Self is the same Self as yours. Obviously you have different minds. However, that is irrelevant except for the purposes of argument.

I am not talking about communication here. Communication is a process in which people become clear with each other for the purpose of making life together satisfying. I am talking about argument, in which the purpose is to make the other person wrong. Arguments are not necessarily loud or abusive. They may be quite composed and subtle. Communication, on the other hand, is not necessarily subtle and polite. Whether what you have is a communication or an argument depends on your intention or lack of it. The content of a discussion does not determine your intention in the discussion. In arguments the purpose is to dominate others, make them wrong, and control them. It doesn't work, but never mind that. The purpose of a communication is to create satisfaction in the relationship. You can totally shout a person down and, if you are coming from communication, it will all work out. You can be as reasonable as hell and if your purpose is to argue, it will never work.

If you are in a mind pattern of arguing with people, you are stuck with it until you accept it and acknowledge that you cause it. Until you get with the fact that it isn't good or bad, that there is only this thing called consequences, you are stuck with it. If you think arguing is good you are stuck with it. If you think it is bad you are stuck with it. Whatever you have a judgement (resistance) on, you are stuck with in some form. What you do about arguing is accept it. When you accept it, you will notice that you no longer have this burning desire to be right. In fact, that is the *way* you will know that you have accepted it: it will begin to clear up. This goes for the rest of your "problems," by the way. Next you will notice that you only argue about things you have stuff on anyway. Then you will recall that having stuff on something means that you are dealing with a false cause.

Then notice that your survival does not depend on being right and "winning" arguments. At that point you are cause in the matter of arguments and you are then at choice. Notice that arguing doesn't work, that it requires your participation (one person can't argue alone), then communicate if you have anything to communicate. If you don't, then be silent. It is OK, I promise you, to be silent or just be.

Finally, there is this belief that arguments are inevitable, which you must give up in order to experience arguments out of your universe. As long as you keep that belief as a truth, you cannot be at cause in your arguments and you cannot have choice about whether to stop or continue. Arguments are *not* inevitable. You do not have to argue. You do not *have* to argue. There is no diabolical force in the universe that forces you to argue. The idea that there is is a cosmic joke and I find it amusing and enlightening. And enlightenment is the condition in which not only do arguments not take place, they are not even appropriate, nor are they ever thought of. The world may lie in darkness, but you don't have to.

Chapter Fourteen:
Addiction

Addiction to a substance is a physical representation of all that you have disowned in your life and will not be responsible for putting there.

Addiction is a mind condition that consists of a strongly ingrained belief that you will not survive without some particular substance. The purpose of an addiction is to extinguish all or part of your experience of the events in your life. This can be anything outside of the real survival needs: air, nutriments, and love. You can make even one of these an addiction if you develop a belief that you need more to survive than you actually do. In the case of air we call the condition hyperventilation. In the case of nutriments: obesity. And in the case of love: dependent personality. Practically any substance can be used in an addiction pattern. Almost everyone has an addiction in some form. If you are not aware of an addiction in your life you are probably unconscious of it. Addiction is incredibly common. Most of us think of addiction in a right/wrong, good/bad frame of reference. Addiction is none of these and there are consequences.

Addiction to a substance is a physical representation of all that you have disowned in your life, all that you will not be responsible for putting there. The substance may come to serve one of two functions: (1) it may be used to anesthetize away that which you have disowned, and/or, (2) it may come to be conceptualized by the mind as the source of that which you have disowned. These are common occurences with addiction but

118

they don't *have* to occur. Addiction may just sit there in your life, like a frog among princes, and simply not go away. It sticks for powerful reasons. It represents mind structures through unconscious associations. But don't start looking for the unconscious associations. They are there, but understanding them does not put you at choice about addiction. Addiction is not wrong and it is not even a problem *if* you are at choice about it. Almost no one feels at choice about an addiction.

The process of addiction goes more or less like this: disowned responsibility for experience — endowment of responsibility in a substance — creation of beliefs about the substance to justify use of the substance — inappropriate use of the substance. Addiction is then held in place by the need to be right, and the substance assumes extraordinary power in your life. This is actually the power that was once yours which you gave away when you identified yourself as your mind's stuff.

The condition then serves to give you an identity. I don't mean a total identity, although even this can be. But at least a fragment of you is an "addict." You then have something to be ashamed of or, in some cases, proud of. Either way you have an identity of sorts. You may have a built-in club of other addicts. Suddenly there are people in your life. You may get sympathy from those who are not hooked. You have something in common with those who are hooked. There is something to talk about: your addiction (you may call it a "habit") or the other person's addiction (or habit).

Perhaps you are getting a sense that addiction is a game with certain rules and certain payoffs. It is. You may be truly stuck in this game, depending on just how much of your power you have given away. If you want to be at choice about it, I am going to tell you how. Take a look at life and know that it is all going to work out. Nothing is really important. Presidents and kings come and go. War and disease come and go. Saints and sages are born and die. Great migrations have swept whole races across the world. And it has always worked out. It always will too. Anything else you have to say about it, whether it was good or bad, right or wrong is just some inconsequential stuff your mind made up one day when it was unwilling to be bored. Inconsequential in that all that stuff your mind says about it doesn't change anything. It is still the way it is. Isn't it the way it is? Of course it is! Always has been. Always will be. Now I want you to take a look at your addiction. If war, disease, kings, and countries all come and go, is your addiction important? What's that you say? Important to you? I didn't ask that! I asked if it was important. Is it? Of course not. Any fool can see that it's not important, your little (or big) habit. Now, if you can *experience* that it is not wrong, here is what happens.

You already know that it is OK to not be addicted, right? Now you know that it is OK to be addicted, *if* that is your experience *when* it becomes your experience. By the way, it won't be your experience until it is. When it is, you have a condition existing within the framework of what is OK, called addiction/no addiction. In that instant a miracle occurs. You are at choice. You can now choose to play a game called no addiction. This game is effortless. There is no struggle involved. You simply do what works to be in the condition of no addiction. If there is a struggle involved you are not at choice, which means that you didn't get the point about it not being important. You may also choose to keep your substance use and it will all work out; we will all live until we die.

Chapter Fifteen:
Choice Of Your Life's Work

Choose your life's work to manifest your purpose in being here, then do what you do with fire and abandon. Contribute. Be satisfied.

This chapter is about the process of becoming. Most of us go toward what we think we want to do in our lives more or less in reverse. What I mean by that is that mostly you go after what you think you want to do without the experience that is necessary to really do what you do well. The experience that is missing is that of actually being whoever it is that does whatever it is you want to do. So we are about to look at the abstractions that allow you to really do what you do with total abandon, so that the job gets done and you get satisfaction.

First we must back up a step and acknowledge that no one is anything and everyone is everything. By that I mean that no one is born with a specific identity in life. The human infant has limitless potential in every direction, but no pre-determined vocational identity. When you take form in a body, you obligate yourself to accumulate the characteristics that identify you in the world as different from others. Part of these characteristics relate to what you do for a living and to contribute to the world.

People work at what they do for two purposes, both totally legitimate. The first purpose is to survive. If you don't survive there is no "what you do next" to make a contribution. So you had better survive. The unfortunate truth is that many of us never get beyond this level. Even millionaires sometimes do not graduate to the next level, the level of contribution. It's ironic, too, because the next level is really why people stick around. I have never seen a person who, under all the fear of not surviving, did not want to make a contribution to others and the world. However, the fear of not surviving drives the basic desire to contribute into unconsciousness. The resurrection of contribution depends on handling your survival fears.

If you are reading this you have survived. I promise you that you know how so well that if you took your attention off survival you would still survive. When you do get your attention off survival, you can experience the process of becoming. The process of becoming involves giving something up. What you must give up is your sense of infinite potential in all directions. You will always have this potential, but you can't manifest it. There isn't enough time in your life to do that. You can only manifest that which you manifest. If you are unwilling to give up the desire to be everything, that is, manifest *all* of your potential, you won't be able to manifest any of it. So if you become a plumber, that means you give up being a carpenter, mechanic, physician, politician, and about a thousand other things you have the potential for; that is that you could become.

Now, notice that word "become." Contained in this word is all you need to know about choosing and doing your life's work. Simply turn it around and read it as "coming to be." This is the essence of becoming anything. First you create the experience (out of nothing) that you be it. You *are* "it," by the way, since you start with infinite potential in all directions. After you have thoroughly created the experience of being "it," or coming to be, the next step comes naturally, without effort. You can only have the experience of "being" whatever-it-is if you also know that you don't have to be it. This is our old friend choice. Choice is selection from cause after you have considered the reasons for and against, but not derived out of the reasons. Again: choice is selection from *cause*. The cause is *you*. You choose whatever-it-is freely, knowing you don't have to. That is, if you don't, you will still survive. You must also accept the fact that when you choose one thing, you unchoose a lot of other dreams you have had.

When you take the first step, the next one follows naturally without effort, as night follows day. You *do* whatever it is you are does in the process of being it. This focuses the houselights on your intention. If you truly choose what you choose, then your intention manifests itself through your doing what you do when and where you say you will do it. This is called keeping your agreements. Keeping your agreements focuses on your intention and your integrity. Remember you *always* get what you intend whether you like it or not. That is the nature of intention. Manifesting integrity in agreements is a function of your intention to become what you say you want to become.

The next step is too simple to merit much attention. You get to have whatever it is that what you are brings by doing what it does. In other words, you get the just rewards of your labor.

There is a final step which most people overlook. Even if you go through with becoming, doing, and having, you are not guaranteed satisfaction in it. You are the cause of satisfaction or the lack of it. *Nothing* will make you satisfied. Satisfied is a way you choose to be or not to be. What is ordinarily referred to as satisfaction comes to us through two channels: work and love. We have just finished talking about work; now we will take a look at love.

Chapter Sixteen:
Love

Love is the fundamental relatedness in the universe, which is just the way it is. You can experience that to the degree that you are willing to come from it and not try to take possession of it.

The experience of love is ordinarily thought of in terms of romantic notions. Love definitely exists at the romantic level, and when it does it involves creating someone in your experience as being perfect the way he or she is. The way they are includes the way they are changing. So romantic love is also a continuous re-creation of the experiential perfection of another person as the other person changes form and content. Romantic love is a large confrontation for the mind which thrives on fault finding. Nevertheless, the power of the Self which you possess is such that, when you choose to, you can love a person at the romantic level indefinitely. To create someone as perfect in your experience, it is necessary to look through and beyond the stuff in your mind *and* in her or his mind. And there is an even more fundamental aspect of love than this.

There is a fundamental relatedness in the universe which is just the way it is. It is the force that holds matter and Self together at all levels from atomic to cellular to non-physical. You don't have to do anything to make it so. It is so, always has been, and always will be. In fact, there isn't anything you can do to reverse this condition. So, if you happen to not like it or have some opinions that it shouldn't be that way, there is nothing you can do about it.

This fundamental relatedness comes from the fact that we all came from the same everything/Nothing. We are *apparently* individuals for now. Apparently, Nothing- or Context-decided to play a game with its Self, and here we are. It won't last long.

In the meantime we have glimpses of the fundamental out of time, place, and thing experience of relatedness that we have called "love." This usually occurs with another person and always involves communication, that is, recreating the experience of another. At that instant, which exists not in time, we love *and* know it. After the actual experience of love a mind condition hangs on which is left behind as a memory trace of the experience. This mind condition is pleasant in itself until it becomes enmeshed with the mind structures.

The actual experience of love, then, occurs in no time and the mind attempts to bring it into time and freeze it in place so as to preserve and enjoy it. It doesn't work. Too bad. Like everything else, when you resist the condition of no love it just persists.

What you must realize about love is that it is always there. That doesn't mean that you always experience it. What it means is that it is always there to be experienced. To the degree that you can give up your chase for it, you can have it. The barrier to the experience of love is the mind. Let me remind you that the mind is that organ that consists of all of your physicality, the purpose of which is to survive itself. It will do anything to survive itself, except that on some occasions it will choose to be right rather than survive. Its techniques for survival are domination and manipulation through being right at all times. The mind lives in abject fear that it will not survive, and practically everything is evaluated by the mind in terms of its survival value. Pain has negative survival value as far as the mind is concerned and pleasure has positive survival value.

So, along comes the experience of love, incredibly pleasurable. The mind latches onto it, immediately makes a memory out of it, tries to stick close to *who it thinks* the source was, and generally botches things up by being right and sticking the "love object" with demands for faithfulness.

The source of love is not the other person. The source of love is not even who you are accustomed to thinking you are. Love, or fundamental relatedness, is the way the universe is. You may experience it to the degree that you are willing to come from it and not try to take possession of it. You don't have to go out looking for it. It isn't some "where." It is everywhere. Love is a guest who will visit your house when she doesn't have to, and *only* when she doesn't have to. You can't demand a visit and get it.

[In fact, you have to be in the condition of enlightenment as well in order to experience frequent visits from love. By the way, frequent visits, that take no time, are the best you can ever hope for. In between visits you get to just be and accept being. Unless, of course, you don't accept just being, in which case love's visits will be very rare.]

Most people come from the context of insufficiency when it comes to love. What I mean about that is that you *say* that there isn't much fundamental relatedness in the universe and you had better not give yours away lest you not have any left or give only a little to the "right" people at the "right" times, under the "right" conditions. The appropriate context for love is the context of sufficiency. Within this context you can begin to experience the truth about love. The truth is that you don't have to hoard it. I invite you to the context in which you can actually give away *all* you have and still have an infinite amount left to give away. It is yours *only* if you give it away.

Finally, I want to say a few words about love and need. "Need" is that condition you are in when you think you must have a certain something to survive which you don't actually have to have. Love *is* something you must have to survive, but you don't have to have it from a *particular* person. If you get stuck thinking that you do, there is one person in the world whom you cannot have love you: it is the person you need. You can't love or be loved by what you need. Also, love can exist very well in the absence of fulfillment of needs. Love is quite powerful and can exist in the absence of sex, physical presence, financial support, and anything else you can name. Love is the one thing that even time can't erase. It is who you are and where you come from.

A popular place you can experience love is in relationship. So, next we are going to look at relationships.

Chapter Seventeen:
Relationships

Relationship is that without which you cannot
have the experience that you exist.

Life is about discovering one's Self. All the games you have set up in your life are about finding and experiencing your Self. Even the game of survival is designed so that you can stick around and experience your Self. There is something to know about experiencing your Self: it can only be experienced in relationship. Relationship can include the relationship you have with rocks, trees, animals, and the elements. However, here we will discuss relationship as it exists with another person, the primary source of your experience of Self.

Go with me on an imaginary trip. This trip begins in Nothing, which as you know is nowhere. You are actually going to make this trip alone although I will be your guide. You are going to come out of nothing and enter a world where there are no living creatures, not even plants. You are going to take a living form, much like the one you have now, except that you will be totally alone. Now that I have guided you to this world devoid of life, I am going to leave you and you will forget who brought you. You will not only not be with anyone, you won't even remember being with anyone. Now, sit back and experience what life is like on this planet.

If you are very conscious, you will be able to perceive that on this forsaken planet you have no idea that you exist. There is absolutely no one and no thing to validate you, or even tell you that you are there. You are going to live out your life in this condition. The parts of your body seem as irrelevant as the rocks around you. Your sex drive is a total mystery to you. You have no idea of what vision is, although your eyes see some things. You are confused by the few sounds you hear. You have no idea of the purpose of anything you have. If you had a language to think in (which you don't), you might think that life is not worth living. But you don't even know you are alive, so that never occurs to you. Your body changes as the years pass and eventually you die, not knowing that you lived. Your only relationships were at the absolute physical level where, when you bumped a rock, it moved.

I have painted a picture of no relationship to give you a sense of what relationship is all about. Relationship is about experiencing your Self. But there is a hook in the system: you cannot directly experience another Self because you are stuck with your physicality. Therefore, you will have to experience and express your relationships through your machine. Your machine has (is) a mind that likes to survive and be right. Already you have a large block to the experience of the Self. So your relationships will fall into several categories, depending on how much survival is at issue. These levels are as follows: (1) ABSTRACTIONS, (2) FRIENDS, (3) LOVERS, (4) WORKERS, (5) SLAVE/MASTER.

Relationship at the level of abstractions is like the one you and I have. It is easy to experience a basic relatedness at this level because there aren't many mind structures in the way. My experience is that I love you. At the level of abstractions, that is all there is. I don't mean ideas and concepts. Ideas and concepts reside in the mind, and if you have been reading this book with only your mind you will have to think this is all some bad craziness about my loving you. You see, abstractions are those laws that run the universe. Gravity is an abstraction. Every time you let an object go, it moves toward the body in the universe which combines the aspects of size and closeness, in your case, the earth. So if you notice the abstraction called gravity (which someone noticed for the first time only a few centuries ago), you can then get in tune with the universe and avoid walking off cliffs and the like. This book is about abstractions which generate the conditions of your life as surely as gravity generates falling.

Add physical proximity and you are dealing with the elements of abstraction *plus* fulfillment of one of your survival needs: love. People at this level are known as "friends." Your mind goes to work overtime figuring out if this person can be "trusted," that is, not say or do anything that falls outside of your belief systems. Depending on the strength you give your belief systems, you may have few or many friends whom you can "really trust," as you say.

Add the element of sex and presto! You are at the level of lovers. Your mind really gets down to work now, judging and evaluating, and you have another opportunity to confront your mind and transcend it. Add the element of survival and you have marriage, in which people depend on each other to bring home the bacon. The mind becomes extremely active in this relationship, judging, evaluating, developing opinions and positions, believing and having faith. Relationship at this level is a wonderful opportunity to experience what you are bigger than.

Take away the element of sex and leave in the element of survival, and you are at the level of workers. How well you work with people determines how well you survive and, sometimes, *if* you survive. Working is a large challenge, equal to marriage in the opportunity it provides to make your life work. What works at this level, ironically, is to forget that survival is an issue and get with your real purpose for being on the planet: to serve others. If you do this at work you will shortly be running your organization, I promise you.

Slave/master relationships are created to further the survival of one person at the expense of the aliveness of another. Both parties are totally plugged into survival in slave/master relationships. There is no space for satisfaction on either side. These types of relationships are officially obsolete but persist in unofficial forms to this day. If you have one, get rid of it. Life is too short.

There is another thing for you to know about relationships. This is the matter of leaving patterns. Generated out of the unwillingness to be responsible for your experience of a person will come up another solution to your made-up problems that what to do about it is to leave. So I want you to know some things about leaving people. It is fine to do so. Not wrong. And there are consequences. The consequences are that you take your "stuff" to the next relationship you have and recreate your experience. You then have another opportunity to become responsible for your experience of people. At that point you can come into responsibility or you can leave again. If you leave, the cycle repeats and you get another opportunity. Sooner or later you will realize, maybe, only if you do, that the source of your unpleasant experience of people is you. The alternative to leaving is to become larger than the leaving pattern of your mind. This gives you an opportunity to experience that you are more than the sum of the parts of your mind. Until you are willing to confront your experience of people, you are in a little prison within your mind which you may be disguising as "freedom." You are stuck feeling as small as you believe you are or (in the event that you *really* are not responsible), as small as you believe the other person is. I invite you to stay in your relationships, become responsible for your experience of them, and find out that even you are large enough to make your life satisfying without making others wrong.

A further thing for you to know about relationships is that you don't have to "try" or work to make them happen. If you have a dearth of relationships in your life what you need to do is not *more*, but less. You need to stop doing those things that prevent natural relationships from happening in your life. Relationship is the natural order of things. If you are not satisfied with the ease with which relationships happen for you, become conscious of what you do to prevent that natural process and stop. If you need assistance in becoming conscious, people will provide assistance to you when they experience that you are ready to get off being right about the way you act, or present yourself, so that you can get their communication.

Finally, I want you to know that human beings exist in their minds. Since this is the condition that we are in, "stuff" always comes up in relationships, sooner or later. Judgements are passed. You notice that there are features that you don't like in the other person. They won't believe as you do. They will have different interests. If you stick in a relationship long enough, *any* relationship, these things will come up. Every time. This is where commitments come in. You see, when the inevitable happens, you will want to leave. Your leaving patterns will be activated. You will go through a stereotyped machine-like process that is characteristic for your particular mind, the end result of which is for you to leave and feel justified. I invite you to be bigger than that. Your mind stuff is really not important, but you will never know that until you stick around long enough to experience it. This sort of commitment is called: "No matter what comes up out of my mind or yours, I am not leaving." Coming out on the other side is the only way you will ever experience your bigness, your Self which transcends your identity in this world.

Chapter Eighteen:
Love Relationships That Work

Powerful love relationships are not generated in the mind. You will have to do it, since your machine can't. You can do it when you are willing to surrender and be surrendered to. You have to be out of your mind.

Some love relationships are remarkable in the degree of power and love generated. Powerful love relationships reach out and make it possible for other relationships to work. This kind of relationship has several features in common which are worth knowing about. The most important thing to know about them is that they occur naturally, without effort. They are generated out of Nothing and as such are not like those relationships created through the mind. Because the mind is not involved in a powerful love relationship, the generating conditions of the relationship are not ordinarily available to the participants at the conceptual level. Therefore, people who have a powerful love relationship usually cannot explain to you how they do it. They *can* give you how they *think* they did it, but it almost always turns out that they are as mystified about how it came to be the way it is as anyone else.

Therefore, I am going to tell you how they do it, so you will know. Before I do, I want you to know that your mind won't like it. It will contradict some of the basic conditions of your mind. So, knowing you won't like it, here it is. One or both persons surrenders to the purposes of the other's life. By "surrenders" I mean that you take the other person's purposes as your own and give up yours. You give up yours so completely that "yours" is not even the appropriate word to use for your former purposes. What this produces is alignment of purpose. Alignment of purpose is the condition out of which powerful love relationships are formed. It has nothing to do with likes or dislikes, how good looking they are, or music, books, perfume, or any of that stuff you thought it did. If you are stuck at this level in relationships, that is, if you think these things are important, you don't have a chance of creating a powerful love relationship.

In most cases there is a power-giver and a power-receiver. The power-giver is the person who surrenders to the life purposes of the power-receiver. The power-receiver experiences absolutely no pride in having power and always remembers from whom it came. The person who surrenders and gives away power does so without conditions. Nothing the receiver can do will result in the loss of power. The receiver then takes this power and uses it to manifest the relationship in perfection. The content of the relationship is held in a context of joy. Both people are nurtured and enlivened in their experience of the relationship, and it exists in a condition of commitment and loyalty. The result is that the relationship is *much* more than the sum of its parts. The power of the relationship enlivens all those with whom it comes in contact. It actually generates the conditions for others to have the same relationship.

Although the relationship is generated out of Nothing, it always contributes *something* to the world. Not a particular something, simply something of value to others. The power that the relationship generates beyond the sum of its parts thrusts out into the world and is given away. The more it is given away, the more there is available in the relationship. Usually the power-receiver is the *apparent* conduit through which power is given away to the world in the form of contribution to the lives of others. However, this is only the apparency. Remember that the power-giver is the power source. All contribution to the world from the relationship can be traced back to its power source.

I want to emphasize that this is the *natural* condition of love relationships. You have to do something with your mind mechanisms to prevent manifestation of a powerful love relationship. Here are the ways to prevent a working powerful love relationship from being manifested. First, if you are the power source, give the receiver your power on the condition that it be used in a certain way or else you will take it back; that is, withdraw your support. Or be *proud* about your terrific relationship and be sure to let others know that you are better than they are for having it. That will do it every time. If you are the power-receiver, use the power to the ends of your mind. Make yourself right through the use of your power. Argue and make others wrong. Don't communicate. Be unwilling to be satisfied with your position in the relationship as power-giver or receiver. If you are the person who have been given power, forget where it came from and don't acknowledge source. These are only a few of the many ways to prevent your relationship from being powerful, nurturing, and contributing. An inventive mind can dream up other ways.

It is not righteous to have such a powerful relationship. It is simply another way of being, and it works for those who choose it. But, however you are in a relationship is OK. If it's not, you are stuck in it until you realize that you aren't wrong.

Finally, I want you to know that you don't have to go out looking for a new person to create a powerful love relationship. All people are basically the same when *you* reach a condition of responsibility. The one you have right now will do just fine. It may be that for you to create a powerful working relationship with the person you are with now, you have something to give up. What you may have to give up are all of the relationships with other people that *could* be. Not only that, you must give up your *dreams* about those other relationships that could be. And I promise you that those relationships *could* be. You have to know that in order to really be in the relationship you have now and be at cause in the matter. The searching from relationship to relationship in this world is powered by two factors: (1) the yen for the "perfect one" (who doesn't exist), and (2) a rejection of yourself that is manifested in the world as rejection of others.

Once you have transcended these barriers to a powerful working relationship, you will be confronted with the fact that the "find-a-relationship" game is over with and it will be up to you to create the purpose of your relationship, that is, a new game to replace the "find-a-relationship" game. If you don't create a purpose, you will find yourself back in the old game called "find-a-relationship" which appears, and is, rather inappropriate after you already have a relationship. Nevertheless, this is the natural outcome of relationships without purpose.

When all of these barriers are passed, the final thing that will be up for you within your relationship will be maintaining yourself and the other person in a condition of loyalty. The next chapter deals with this topic.

Chapter Nineteen:
Loyalty And Acknowledgement

Loyalty is that condition in a relationship which allows you to contribute to the purpose of the relationship at cause. Acknowledgement is the space in which loyalty exists.

It is appropriate to discuss loyalty and acknowledgement together for without acknowledgement, loyalty cannot exist for long. Loyalty is that condition in a relationship that allows you to contribute to the purpose of the relationship at cause. When you contribute to something at cause, it doesn't cost you anything. That is, there is no "sacrifice" involved, in fact you gain from it. In the condition of loyalty you know clearly that when you contribute to the purpose of a relationship you are actually contributing to yourself. The purpose can also be that of a family, an organization, or the world.

There is something curious about loyalty. There is something that must be in order for loyalty to endure: it must be noticed. The contribution that is made in the condition of loyalty must actually be noticed and acknowledged. If you simply remember that no one *owes* you anything, loyalty will be easy for you to notice and acknowledge. If you begin to think that "they" owe you loyalty, you are in for trouble. If you have an employee who is making a contribution and you want to keep that person, what you do is acknowledge him, his contribution, and his loyalty. If you don't let him know that you are aware of his importance in your life and your organization, you won't have that person very long. If you have a wife who really serves you in life and you want her to have the freedom to stay in a condition of loyalty to the relationship, what you do is let her know that she powers your life with her loyalty. If you don't, you may wake up single one morning.

So loyalty requires acknowledgement in order to exist over time. No acknowledgement is necessary for the generation of loyalty. People can do that out of Nothing with no support. We are speaking here about the *maintenance* of loyalty. I am simply telling you what works. You don't have to go apply it. You may not intend to have loyalty in your life. If that is the way it is for you, you will demonstrate it by not acknowledging people in your life.

What about the flip side of the issue? What if it is *your* condition of loyalty and it is waning due to the fact that no one seems to notice your contribution? What to do? If you are going to live your life at cause, this is a perfect opportunity for you to begin to see that you are not the effect of anyone other than yourself. You can create your own acknowledgement, first by doing a good job at whatever you do. Then, if you aren't noticed, you will know that your intention is not up for creating acknowledgement. When you get your intention up you will do whatever is appropriate to create the acknowledgement you want. It isn't selfish to want acknowledgement, by the way. The purpose of being acknowledged is to have the conditions in which you can continue to be loyal and do a good job. So, for example, if you are someone's terrific husband and not getting credit for it, you are responsible for creating the conditions and the circumstances in which you can and will be acknowledged.

Now, I do not mean, necessarily, spoken acknowledgement. And it may be spoken, or even written. But it doesn't have to be verbal. It can be as non-verbal as a wave of the hand. Ultimately, it all depends on your ability and willingness to acknowledge yourself. If you do that, you will notice that others are already acknowledging you right and left. If you don't acknowledge yourself, no amount of praise will be "enough" to satisfy you. So, you see, it all comes back to you. You are the source of your experience. You are responsible, not only for getting what you want, but also for experiencing it as well. And no one can make you. It isn't even right to create being noticed and praised. It simply allows you to continue functioning well in life.

I want to be sure that you know that loyalty is the *natural* condition in life. People are just naturally loyal to each other. You have to do something, or omit something by intention to create a condition of disloyalty. You have to put some "stuff" on it. You have to judge it, criticize it, or not notice. You have to actively drive loyalty out of being, and it isn't easy. You have to be really skilled and tenacious to do it.

Finally, I want you to know that no one owes you loyalty. You can't do enough to deserve it. It is a free unconditional gift that comes out of the fact that there is a basic relatedness in the universe which is just the way it is. If you don't have loyalty in your life, you threw it away. If you do have it, be sure to remember that no one owes it to you. While you are remembering, be certain to let whoever is loyal to you know that you appreciate their gift. Loyalty is simply too great a gift to deserve.

This is the end of the book about your life working. Now it begins. What begins is your life working with you in the experience of that. You see, your life is already working. Your experience of everything in your life has turned out the way you intended it to turn out. To experience that, take responsibility for it. When you actually reach that level of responsibility you will realize that what has always been just under that is an incredibly strong desire to see the world work at the level of responsibility and satisfaction. The next book is about your taking responsibility for that as well.

BOOK FOUR: ENLIGHTENMENT AT THE LEVEL OF THE WORLD

This is your world.
Your world is run by ideas.
You are the source of ideas.

Chapter One:
Evil From Source

You can't be any bigger than you are willing to acknowledge being small.

It could be said that evil is the sacrifice of aliveness in relationship in order to be right. I am not interested here in informing you that evil exists in the world. I am certain that you know that. I want to expand evil to the level of abstraction that allows it to begin to come to a natural end. Anything expanded to the appropriate level of abstraction dissolves, except for the basic laws which run the universe. Gravity, for example, will not dissolve at the level of absolute abstraction because it is itself an absolute abstraction. Abstraction (like gravity) generates experience (like "things are falling"), and experience in turn generates mind. That is just the reverse of what you have been taught, which is that mind generates experience which generates abstraction. However, abstractions do not depend on your experience to exist. So the proper sequence is abstraction, experience, mind. Then mind generates concept, which is the way it puts together or "understands" abstraction. But concept is not abstraction. They stand at diametrically opposite poles. Evil, like concept, is generated by mind. There is no abstraction in the universe called "evil." In fact, evil cannot exist at the level of abstraction, much less at the level of Nothing, which generates abstraction.

Evil will persist as long as it is resisted. The resistance to evil is basically the holding it in the context of being "bad." I do not

143

include the *consequences* of evil in the "resistance" to it. The consequences are simply the consequences. *Resistance* is that which causes evil to persist. In other words, the law is the law. The law is not "resistance" and has nothing to do with the persistence or non-persistence of evil, as you may have noticed. What allows, even enables, evil to persist is the righteous judgements that we lay on it. That is the fuel supply evil uses to run its motor. In other words, it is our unwillingness to confront the source of evil: our own mind. This circumstance allows evil to persist.

Individual perception of evil is curious. From the vantage point of the mind, evil exists always on the "outside" of the mind. This should come as no surprise to you, as you know that the mind thinks it survives by making itself right. To do this it defines evil in such a way that it will not have to confront it. Since the definition the mind gives for evil doesn't work to cause it to disappear, let's take a closer look at what it is. Then we will look at the definition that will expand evil to the level of abstraction, which allows it to disappear. The mind's definition of evil is: anything anyone does (perhaps even thinks) which falls significantly outside what the mind believes is right. This definition works to make people wrong, and when written into law and enforced it works to incarcerate people. Unfortunately, it does nothing to cause evil to disappear. What *is* evil really? I mean, what is the definition that represents the truth and allows evil to be and disappear?

Evil is any thought intended to exclude any individual or group of individuals, so as to justify the doing of something to that individual or group which does not promote their aliveness and enhance their experience of worth. It is the selling out of aliveness in order to be right and make others wrong. Note that it is the *thought* which is evil, not the doing. It is the *judgement*, if you will, which precedes the doing and which justifies the doing. "Doing," by the way, includes not doing in some cases when a withheld word or deed is withheld for the purpose of making another wrong, not promoting aliveness or enhancing their experience of worth. This definition is derived out of a fundamental abstraction which is accurately stated thus: "You can't be any bigger than you are willing to acknowledge being small." When you elevate evil to this level of abstraction it begins to disappear in your experience of life.

However, the mind cleverly defines evil where it is not ("out there") to allow it to persist where it is ("in here"). Any time you make another person wrong, you have created evil and prepared the way for the overt acting out of that evil. You may choose not to act it out yourself. Perhaps you will encourage others, or even society, to act it out for you.

So, is evil bad? No, it's just evil. Is what you do, or encourage others to do, bad? No, and there are consequences. You see, you really can't do bad things to other people. You can only do bad things to yourself. The external appearance may be that you have harmed another. They will get over it. You won't. You will carry it around for the rest of your life. You can deny it, justify it, ignore it, and it will still be there. Is that bad? No. It's simply nature's way of preserving itself. If you do enough of it you will begin to not sleep well. A little more and other body disorders will appear. Do enough, and you will be in a state of living death. So, is that bad? No. Does it work to make yourself wrong for the evil you have done? No. As usual, making yourself right or wrong doesn't work. You will just have to be bigger than the mistakes you have made.

It just so happens that all evil is legal within the law. We can't punish you for something you think. It also happens that most of what you decide to act out of your evil is also within the law. Making others wrong is not illegal in most forms.

We have gone through this discussion of evil so that you will have a context to hold evil in as we discuss the various forms in following chapters. I can't emphasize to you too much that the old context called "evil is bad" doesn't work to disappear evil. The new context called "evil is and there are consequences" works when you take responsibility for it. This is another level from the responsibility you take for your own life. Obviously you can't move to this level until you have handled it at the personal level. You can't wait around for someone else to handle the world. It won't happen. You may ask, why me? Well, why not you? Just be willing to consider the possibility that this is the beginning of an age and that you happen to be living at the start of it. So, you have the privilege of ushering in the age of enlightenment. But, why now? Why not now? It must happen some time and this is it. I must tell you again that in order to experience the age of enlightenment you must take responsibility for it. If the whole world became enlightened and you remained endarkened, *your* world would still lie in darkness. If you become enlightened at the level of the world you can experience what is, at world level. I don't mean you to take this as an airy concept. Literally, for the world to become enlightened *you* personally must take responsibility for it. Not as a burden, but as a privilege. After all, this is your world. The most evil thing you can do is withhold your love from it.

Chapter Two:
Racism

Biologically speaking, there is no "race" except at the local track meet.

Let's not mess around. Let's take on a biggy right now. Mankind has played a cruel joke on itself by exercising the ability to adapt skin color to climatic conditions. There are certain areas of the world where the intensity of sun exposure renders survival difficult for white-skinned people. Man, the consummate survivor, naturally figured a way around being fried by the sun. Merely disperse the melanin pigment of the skin evenly, and develop a bit more of it, and presto! Automatic protection from the sun.

Nature did this much. The mind of man did the rest. Of course skin color isn't the only physical characteristic humanity uses to divide itself, but it serves admirably to demonstrate a principle. Biologically speaking, there is no "race," except at track meets. Race is a false concept invented by the mind of man for the purpose of dominating and manipulating others. The specific location of "race" within the mind is in that part known as "belief systems." A belief exists that there is a *natural* division of people. Resting on this belief is a system of justification making it OK to segregate some from others. Further justification makes it OK to think of the other race as naturally inferior or naturally "red-necked," or whatever. Both of these are positions or points of view. So the structure goes like this: the foundation stone is a belief called " 'Race' is a natural condition." This belief supports the justification "There is a natural division of human-kind." This gives rise to a point of view called "They are naturally the way they are." This point of view then makes it possible to prepare people for mistreatment by segregation. At that point, the whole thing surfaces and mistreatment is called "mistreatment." The important thing to realize here is that mistreatment could not occur without its supporting structure.

A diagram will lend clarity:

(Read from the bottom up)

Mistreatment	is	Mistreatment.
Preparation	is	Segregation.
Point of View	is	They are naturally the way they are.
Justification	is	There is a natural division of humankind.
Belief	is	"Race" is a natural condition.

This process can easily be applied to other areas of human relationships wherein people are mistreated. And the root of it all is a mind condition, namely, a belief. This belief is so ingrained that for many people there is no such thing as questioning it. It is a perfect example that the mind defines and shapes what we ordinarily think of as reality. None of us are above it. You do it too. Even you.

The truly unfortunate aspect of belief systems is that they tend to provoke equal and opposite belief systems in others. Racism provokes counter-racism. Counter-racism provokes counter-counter-racism, and so on. To be effective, opposition to racism must have as its purpose to expose racists to themselves, *not* make them wrong. Making them wrong only entrenches them in their condition. You see, people are stuck believing that they are as small as they seem. Making them feel even smaller does not work. I am not speaking only of racism, although this all applies to racism; I am speaking here of principles that transform and enlighten our world.

Underlying even a belief such as " 'race' is a natural condition" is the ground of being that we are the contents of our minds, that there is no way we can ever be more than the sum of our parts. This is the base lie that endarkens the world. You know, you can give up being a racist and you will still be who you are. Your life will still be naturally valuable. You will survive. The world will not end. And you can still contribute to it. After you become responsible for *your* beliefs about "race," what will be up for you is the world condition. The way you can transform the world in this regard is to get off your racism. This gives others an opportunity to get off their racism. Treat people as who they are, not who you believe they are. I promise you that they will be transformed in your experience and often in their experience as well.

Finally, I want you to know the ultimate truth about "race": THERE IS NO SUCH THING.

Chapter Three:
War

War is a giant make-wrong at the level of the world. Enlightenment at the level of the world will end war. Nothing else will.

As long as anyone can remember there have been wars. As far back as history is recorded, wars have been in process, almost continuously. Seemingly, war is a natural condition of man on the planet. Evidently there is no way to stop the occurrence of wars. Big wars, little wars, medium sized wars, everything except no wars. It is a great tragedy of human nature that wars are inevitable. Wars continue because of the politicians. Besides, everyone knows that there isn't enough wealth on the planet and obviously we will have to fight to survive. And so on and so forth.

What you have been reading is the true cause wars continue. Not the actual beliefs presented, but the fact that these beliefs are *held* as the truth. We are up against our old acquaintance belief. Wars continue because of beliefs. As long as there is "no way" that war can end, then there is truly no room in the universe for the end of war as a human endeavor. (The same goes for arguments at the personal level, by the way.) You see, war is a production of the mind. It only *looks* as though it is a production of generals and guns. War is the perfect environment for the unenlightened mind since the mind thrives on making itself right, others wrong, and surviving (except that in war *sometimes* we see that the mind would rather be right and not survive). War

150

is a giant make-wrong at a societal level. Enlightenment at the level of the world will end war. Nothing else will.

The generating condition of war, aside from the unenlightened mind, is the ground of being of insufficiency. This theory has it that there is not "enough" in the world and that what there is must be fought for. So we end up squabbling over food, land, money, oil, etc. Insufficiency, as a ground of being, is manifest in "governments." The purpose of governments in this world is to protect us from each other at the level of nations, organizations, and individuals. This "protection" comes from the theory of insufficiency, wherein I can have mine only at the expense of yours. That is, for someone to profit, someone must take a loss. Within the ground of being of insufficiency, there is no possibility of everyone winning. Someone has to lose. (This also accounts for criminal behavior.)

If we really knew the truth of sufficiency, war, crime, and starvation would be hard pressed to continue existing. Only an enlightened world can generate this condition. I want to remind you that there is *the* world, which you can never know, and there is *your* world, the only one you can know. The world will never begin to look enlightened until your world does. I know that war looks very large to you as an individual. I also want you to know that you are larger than you believe you are and that your life can make a difference.

I have used war to introduce you again to your responsibility for the world which is your world. War is not a thing that is happening "over there." If it is happening anywhere, it is happening in our space. We are infinitely less for it. We will never know the potential of life until we create the context in which war can process itself out of existence. We will always be small while we are destroying each other. And we will always be destroying each other while we are small. The opportunity has always been there to end war; we simply haven't taken responsibility for the opportunity. We have been hiding behind a little belief called "Well, my life is small, and doesn't count." As long as we come from the ground of being that it must be (inevitably), we will never take the responsibility for causing it to disappear, along with slavery.

Feeling guilty about it won't work. What happens if you

begin to feel guilty about it is that war goes on and you feel guilty. Feeling hopeful or hopeless about it won't work either. What will work is the same thing that will work in your personal life: being responsible for it. War is generated out of ideas. We are the source of ideas. Can you imagine what this world could be if we got off of making each other wrong at the level of the planet?

Chapter Four:
Starvation

The most natural thing to do when you are hungry is to feed yourself. People do not die of starvation out of stupidity. They die because we let them die.

Starvation, that is *death* by hunger, now takes the lives of approximately 15 million people each year. I want you to know how many that is. It is about equal to the combined total populations of Dallas, Madison, Denver, Minneapolis, Houston, Atlanta, San Francisco, Oklahoma City, Springfield, Salt Lake City, Phoenix, and New Orleans. It means that 28 human beings die each *minute* from starvation alone. Three-fourths of them are children. The present population of the earth is four billion. This planet has the capacity to support eight to eleven billion. Therefore, your belief that people are starving because of the inability of the earth to support them is not exactly the same thing as truth. The cause of starvation is not what it *seems* to be. The causes of starvation in this world are exactly the same causes of our lives not working at the personal level. They are ideational. Anything else it looks like is only an *apparency*. As long as certain ideas and beliefs are allowed to stand, nothing we do, no matter how expensive, will end starvation.

The first idea is a "no idea." There is no pervasive idea in the world today that people have a *right* to adequate food to maintain their lives. Starving people know there is such a right but they don't stick around to give voice to what they know. A person is no less a person because his or her bowl is empty and yours is full. Nevertheless, the no-idea idea that pervades the world today is that people do not have the right to adequate food to maintain their lives. There *is* an idea that people have a right to free speech and pursuit of happiness. Something has been overlooked, possibly? Now, there is a condition out of which this oversight is generated. That condition is actually a ground of being that is more than where we come from. It is so entrenched that it is, for practical purposes, us. It is a belief that passes unquestioned for truth.

That belief is that there is insufficient food available in the world. Now, if what you want is to end world starvation and you encounter this "truth," then what you do is ditch your intention to end starvation. What you do about it becomes a *gesture* only, and you go on to accomplish what is possible, rather than what is not possible. Immediately you are stuck in a position and people continue to starve due to the "fact" that it is inevitable. Inevitability is the natural outcome of the ground of being of insufficiency. Starvation will exist as long as your position is that it is inevitable. Simple observation, I mean *simple* observation, reveals that it is not inevitable. If it is inevitable, why hasn't everyone of us known someone who starved to death due to lack of food? What's that you say? It is inevitable in some parts of the world and not in others? Yes, and why is that? The truth is that it is not inevitable *and* it is, at least for now, something that we have caused to be.

"But there is nothing I can do, is there?" YES, THERE IS. Get off your positions of inevitability and insufficiency. Now, when you do, the next thing that will come up is that you aren't responsible for it. It is happening in another part of the world, isn't it? I mean, what have you got to do with it? Well, nothing and everything. If you would like to see the world work, let me tell you, it can. However, you can't wait for the rest of the world to become enlightened before you become enlightened. That moment will never come for you. Remember, there is *the* world which you can never know; then there is *your* world, the only one you can know about. You will find that when you become enlightened "the" world becomes enlightened for you. What happens is that your world starts to work and when it does you begin to notice that "the" world is already beginning to work. Until that moment of transformed enlightenment for you, conditions in "the" world, including starvation, appear stuck and hopeless to you. That doesn't mean that they are stuck and hopeless. What that means is that you are stuck hoping *and* hopeless without taking effective action. Remember polarities? The condition that keeps hopelessness stuck in place is its polar opposite: hope. People, like you, are "hoping" that starvation will come to an end. This "hope" serves as a justification for doing nothing or merely gesturing. In this regard "hope" works about as well as "faith" and "charity," both of which call into being their polar opposites.

I see a lot of people in my business and I am an astute observer. And I can tell you, without reservation, what people really want is their world to work. Some need to observe their belly button for a while, or the equivalent in psychotherapy. But, after a bit of that it becomes obvious that their belly-button is in great shape and what is underneath their curiosity about that is their desire for their world to work. It then becomes apparent that personal enlightenment is not separate from enlightenment of the world. You get both or neither. If you want one without the other, you are out of luck. Creating the context of ideas that will allow "the" (your) world to work is the foundation of every life. That *is* your foundation, whether you believe it or not. It doesn't even require your belief. If that were not your foundation, you would be at the opera instead of reading this.

So, within the context of the world working — starvation ending, for example — everything you do works, even what looked like "gestures" of charity before the moment of enlightenment. Before creation of the context of the world working, that is, before the moment of enlightenment, nothing you do works. Everything you do, no matter how valiant, no matter how grand, degenerates into a gesture. So far we have just scratched the surface of what is possible. Starvation is a giant "Go to Hell!" to 15 million people in this world every year. In a very real way it is the same thing to us all. It says that life doesn't count, isn't significant. We can never realize our full potential on the planet until we stop this atrocity. A content of more, better, and different ideas won't work when held in the context of "It can't done." Only an enlightened context will work. It *can* be done and now is the time to seize the opportunity to be responsible for that. Responsibility means a new context in which even the "reasons" it can't be done become a contribution to doing it.

By the way, overpopulation does not cause starvation. Starvation causes overpopulation. In the "Third World" it takes the birth of almost five children to produce one living male heir. A living male heir insures old people someone to care for them in their last years. One must have many children (8–10), when four out of five die of starvation, to insure one living male heir. This is one example of beliefs that take the responsibility for world starvation away from its rightful owners: us.

If we can split an atom, put a man on the moon and a camera on Mars, we can put a meal on the table. Starvation is an opportunity, not a burden.

Chapter Five:
Religion

My intention for your experience of religion is that it become a religion of the Self. That doesn't mean a new church. It means a new context for the church you already have.

Enlightenment of the world is not a new idea. Many others have had it before and accomplished a great deal. The truly gifted masters who created the context for what later became the world's religions had the willingness to let the Self be manifest in the framework of their lives. They were willing to give up and surrender entirely what we ordinarily think of as our "lives" so that there would be space for the manifestation of the Self. Even death held no power over these individuals, for they were truly bigger than their individual life "stories."

However, on the way to what we think is the road to enlightenment we sometimes forget that the requirements for true enlightenment include a willingness to surrender and give up the importance of the "story" of our lives and know that what doesn't endure, isn't. The choices are surrender (or, as I call it here, giving up the importance of the "story") *or* no enlightenment. The condition of no enlightenment takes two forms. "Non-believers" materialize who justify hanging onto their life stories and staying in the pits by saying there is no possibility of anything else. The other form of no enlightenment that appears consists of "believers" who settle for occasional enlightenment in exchange for hanging onto their life story as important or significant. So, with these preliminary comments, I want to tell you how it all came down with respect to religion.

From time to time in life, the mind loses its grip on its domination of the sense modalities and the Self has a direct experience of life, that is, *you* have a direct experience of life. Direct experience of life is extraordinarily pleasurable for the mind and really defies description in words. It seems to give the mind an opportunity not to be for a moment. The occurrence of a direct experience of life is closely related to a phenomenon we call "trust." The condition of trust exists when you know that you are actually going to survive in life, that you are loved, and that you are capable of loving. You are given to and giving. At such a moment your mind releases and the Self is free to experience life directly. This is a universal human experience known by different names in different cultures. Here we call it "enlightenment," however, it is also known as a "religious experience," "being saved," and a "peak experience," among other names. At the moment of enlightenment one knows that there is a part of "me" in everything and a part of everything in "me." One knows by direct experience that time is an illusion and that now is forever.   *ENLIGHTENMENT /PEAK EXPERIENCE*

Then what we call "time" passes, that is, things change, and the direct experience of life is replaced by a return to dominion of the mind. Since the mind's method of surviving is to record and remember, it does just that. It is clear to the mind that something has just happened that was plainly out of its own scope. Since the mind needs to classify things, the closest classification it can think of for what just happened is "pleasure." Being a pleasure seeker, and wanting more than anything to survive itself, the mind makes a memory of the moment of enlightenment and thus seeks to freeze it in "time," that is, prevent it from changing. The mind can't quite grasp that enlightenment happens outside of time. The mind seeks to make itself right by taking credit for the experience. It then begins to tell others what happened and recall what the conditions were when the experience occurred. The mind reasons that the conditions and circumstances surrounding the experience had something to do with the experience itself. The mind then creates beliefs and rituals about those circumstances. The harder the mind tries to recreate the experience, the further away from the experience you are. A sense of frustration sets in and the mind begins to hope and practice rituals. Eventually, the concept of faith sets in. Faith involves a giving up of trying and hoping "it" will happen again. Faith is the highest level below the realm of responsibility and enlightenment. The problem with faith is that it generates new hope, which generates its polar opposite, hopelessness. Beyond faith there is grace, another word for enlightenment.

Religion, then, is a creation of the mind to attempt to set up the conditions for enlightenment to occur. These conditions usually involve certain behavior called rituals, group meetings at the "right" place and the "right" time, exhortations to trust, believe, and have faith.

The difficulty with religion as a ritual is that it freezes life in a condition of hope/hopelessness and no responsibility, no enlightenment. My intention for your experience of religion is that it become a religion of the Self. That doesn't mean a new church. It means a new context for the religion you already have. That context involves becoming responsible for being the source of life and not the effect. It involves a *willingness* to be enlightened whenever you are and an acceptance of the conditions of your mind and the world at every moment. It means living right now. It means clean communicative relationships. It means being true to your life's purpose. It means manifesting your natural integrity. It means satisfaction with and contribution to life. It means that you participate in life by choice. It means that you take responsibility for the way the world is right now and exercise your awesome power in the matter of what the world is becoming. A transformed you means a transformed enlightened world. Have the courage to be enlightened. I can't think of a better place to start than within the framework of your religion.

Chapter Six:
Organizations

*Organizations present us with an enormous
opportunity to make our world work to its potential.*

Any group of two or more people formed for the purpose of getting a particular job done is an organization. This includes everything from one-on-one relationships to governments. What I would like to focus on here is the question of how you can best participate in causing aliveness in your organizations.

A common complaint about organizations is that they do not support and nurture the people within them. People are "kicked out" of organizations for "reasons" which do not exactly nurture anyone *or* promote getting the job of the organizations done.

Individuals can hide easily within organizations, in the sense that responsibility for your experience is easily camouflaged and it is easy to get agreement that a certain thing is so about a person, whether it is or not. Your experience, camouflaged by agreement, then becomes the "reason" for a perpetration on a person that neither assists the person nor the organization to get the job done. This is the mind at work at the level of organization. The degree to which condemnation and perpetration operates in your organization depends on the example you set in your relationship to your organization. To transform your organization you must be responsible for that.

Let us go beyond the individual or, if you like, deeper within ourselves, and see how we prevent organizations from working. Later we will take a look at how to make organizations work. You should take all of the comments I am about to make personally, since blaming others does not help.

There are two ways we prevent our organizations from working: (1) we hold ourselves in a condition of no responsibility for our experience of others, and (2) we come from the ground of being of insufficiency. In the case of the first method, in everyday terms, what this means is that we find our minds in a condition of "not liking" our experience of another person. But, instead of being responsible for our experience, what we say about it is: that is the way they really are. If they are as "bad" as our experience of them, this obviously justifies doing something (a perpetration) to them in the name of the organization. The purpose then, is not for the organization to work. The purpose is to make somebody wrong and hang the organization. In the process, the mind "feels" that it is "better" than some other mind. You would be surprised, or perhaps you wouldn't be surprised, to know how much that passes for organizational activity is actually the right/wrong game. At a larger level we hold ourselves in a condition of no responsibility for our experience of the organization as a whole. We structure our experience in a "me-them" relationship instead of an "us" relationship. Then, when things go awry we say that we are powerless to clean up the operation and isn't it awful (?), instead of using the power we have. Rather than being responsible, we harbor "resentment." Rather than create a condition in which others can express their power, we insist that they keep their ideas to themselves. In a "me-them" relationship you define the organization as an exploiter and yourself as the exploited, and this justifies whatever you care to do to hurt the organization. As you exploit the "exploiter," and this is discovered, you will actually have something done to you which you will use to justify doing something further to the organization. And, as you can see, the process spirals downward.

The ground of being of insufficiency says that there is not enough to go around; you had better get yours or else someone else will. And within this framework, they will. Insufficiency justifies the payment of minimum compensation to members of the organization, which justifies further the already justified attitude that what one should do is the very least possible to still collect the paycheck. Also, what we say is that success, satisfaction, and achievement are in limited supply. This immediately limits what the organization (and individuals within the organization) is willing to be capable of achieving. Once things are thus defined they really begin to look that way. It looks like reality. The people within the organization who can see the truth begin to leave and the process folds in on itself.

Transforming an organization from one that is spiraling downward, not working, is essentially the same as transforming a personal relationship. First of all, you don't need to find a new organization. The one you have now will do fine. You are the source of your relationship with the organization anyway. Then become responsible for your experience of the organization and the people within it. When you do, you will notice that you effortlessly stop blaming others and you feel much lighter about the situation. Know that you are going to survive. Quit feeling threatened until someone actually threatens your life. Then feel threatened. When you develop a "dislike" for someone, don't hide behind the skirts of the organization. Be responsible for your not "liking" someone. Don't pull perpetrations in the name of the good of the organization. After reading this far, surely you are not still of the opinion that your mind's likes and dislikes are significant. But, in case you are, be up front about it. Tell whoever it is you don't like them. Let your mind condition hang out for what it is, so you won't act on it. Remember, anytime you can't admire and respect someone, what that means is that you are afraid that you have got what it is you don't like in them as part of you. In fact, you probably do have those features. And you will continue to have them until you stop resisting them and quit pretending that you don't have them.

Once you have become responsible for your experience of the organization, you are ready to take on the context of insufficiency and replace it with the context of sufficiency. Within the context of sufficiency it becomes OK for everyone within the organization to win. In fact, what this means is that one person within the organization winning represents, and is experienced as, the entire organization winning. The context of sufficiency recognizes the truth: there is plenty in the physical universe. It also eliminates the qualities of pride and shame which prevent organizations working within the context of insufficiency. There is still competition but the cut-throat aspect does not exist. Corrective feedback is given and received as acknowledgement that the job is being handled. It is not given or taken as criticism.

Do you know that it is actually possible to recreate your organization, even yours, so that it not only gets the job done better than before, but that it actually supports and nurtures the individuals who choose to participate in it? And you can do this from any level you happen to be at in the organization. If you really start to communicate effectively, what will happen is that you will be running your organization very soon. Start by supporting those in authority. Give them your power.

[The truth of the matter — that is, what works — is: (1) there is a sufficiency of everything you need for survival; (2) your gain does not come at the expense of someone else's loss, even though it *looks* that way sometimes; (3) *you are* the organization; and as such, (4) your purpose is to nurture yourself by perfecting your experience of the organization. Just as a by-product, the organization is transformed and becomes enlightened. And, of course, you don't have to make it work.]

Organizations present an enormous opportunity for us to make our world work to its potential. In fact, when we enlighten ourselves, the enlightenment of organizations follows automatically. If it doesn't, you really didn't get personal enlightenment yourself and we will have to call it by another name.

Chapter Seven:
Crime

Criminals are an embodiment of a reflex to make-wrongs at the level of society.

We are truly stuck in the problem of crime. It seems that no matter what solution is applied, crime simply increases in prevalence and intensity. More crimes are committed more often. Stricter laws have no effect on the problem of crime. Crackdowns in the central cities merely drive crime to the suburbs. Liberalizing the law doesn't seem to work either. In fact, *everything* has been tried and *nothing* works. What we see out of all this is that our solutions just create new problems. There is obviously something about the context crime is held in which doesn't work. Any solution which is generated in that context will not work. That context is called "criminals are wrong." Even executing criminals seems to inspire others, actually attract others, to commit the same crimes.

Penal systems are set up, not to provide workability to the "criminal justice system," but rather to make the criminal wrong, *very* wrong. It is gratifying to make criminals wrong since they have made us wrong through their crimes. It extracts a measure of revenge from the situation which gives a false sense of justice. People are sent to the most unenlightened places on the earth to become enlightened. They are dealt with by the most unenlightened people in the world and expected to benefit from it. We are truly stuck in the "criminal justice system" which provides no solutions and actually compounds the problems it was designed to solve. Even the term "Judge" sets the stage for the context in which nothing works. People are not dealt with responsibly; they are "judged." There is nothing wrong with this and there are consequences.

Let me pose a few questions. Suppose it were possible for everyone involved in the criminal justice system to come from what works instead of making people wrong. I mean literally everyone, from the arresting officer through the jail keeper, judge, prison officials, and parole officer. What I mean by that is that literally everyone involved drop "judgement" about whether a thing is right or wrong and simply, consistently point out that there are consequences. There is no right or wrong and there *are* consequences. Let me repeat that. The truth is, the *absolute* truth *is*, that there is no right or wrong and there are consequences. The law clearly sets forth the possible consequences of criminal behavior.

You see, what keeps a criminal stuck acting the part of a criminal is the fact that he is made wrong. When you make people wrong, they have to make you wrong, or at least there is a very ingrained tendency to do so. Now, the way a criminal knows to make you wrong is to commit a crime. So, if there is a law against sitting down, the criminal will sit down. If there is a law against standing up, the criminal will stand up. Say "sit down" and he stands up. Say "stand up" and he sits down. The criminal, then, represents or personifies a reflex to make-wrongs. Now, suppose we all got into the truth (this will scare you) and said something like: "Look, there is nothing right or wrong about sitting down and there are consequences, so choose." Some people would choose to break the law, so they would get the consequences. They would get the opportunity to go to jail or pay a fine or whatever. They would go through exactly the same procedures — for example, arrest, arraignment, trial, conviction, lock-up — *except no one makes them wrong*. In other words, the space is given to the person who broke the law which says "Thou shalt not sit down" to be responsible for being the one who did it and got the consequences. Once the price is paid, let us let the price be paid. If we make former criminals wrong for being former criminals, they will make us wrong by being criminals again. It is as simple as that.

So, I am not recommending that we *do* anything differently. What I am recommending is enlightenment, so that we do what we do in the context that works instead of the context that doesn't work. This means nothing more or less than allowing people to be responsible for themselves. Not allowing people to be responsible for themselves creates criminals, irresponsible criminals who have a victim story longer than your arm. Let us at least create responsible criminals so that criminality will have a chance to become boring and obsolete. Let's face it; being a criminal is about the most difficult way there is of getting a job done in life. The very fact that crime exists at all is a testimony to how alluring we make it to the human mind to do things through criminal procedures by making them wrong. You see, crime is not a problem that is "over there" with someone else. It is basic to the condition of the human mind. There is nothing complex about it. Anyone who is alive and awake can comprehend it.

BOOK FIVE:
ADVANCED
ENLIGHTENMENT

This book is for your consideration after you have mastered the previous books experientially as well as conceptually. If you have read and comprehended this far, you are extraordinary and truly in touch with your Self. Nevertheless, the material that has gone before this was to prepare you for this section and future publications. The following material is designed to give you mastery of your life to go along with the understanding that you now have.

Chapter One:
About Having A Teacher

The quality of your life increases directly in proportion to the number of teachers you have in your life.

The purpose of this chapter is to give you an opportunity to get through your judgements of yourself and others about having a teacher. In our world it is very OK to have a doctor, a dentist, a grocer, but you had better not have a teacher or people will think you are weird. What is worse, *you* will think you are weird.

⌈My personal observation is that the quality of my life increases directly in proportion to the number of teachers I can create into my life. I know this to be true for others as well. Why then this taboo against having a teacher? To tell you the truth, there is a conspiracy in the world. The conspiracy (which of course few people will talk about) is to keep it down. What I mean by that is that the purpose of the conspiracy is to keep the quality of the experience of life at a relatively low level. The purpose of keeping a low profile is so that there will always be something just beyond to rise into. Human beings don't know the truth that personal horizons are unlimited. Therefore, there is a fear of reaching "the end" with respect to experience. So, if you have a teacher, people will make you wrong as part of this vast and unconscious conspiracy.⌋

But wait a minute. No one can make you wrong without your cooperation. If you are willing to be large enough (I don't

171

mean gain weight) to not cooperate in making yourself wrong, you can begin to have teachers in your life. You already are large enough for this and the proof is that you are reading this book. Thank you for allowing me to be your teacher. It expands my experience of life and makes it really worth living. Let me assure you of some facts. Having a teacher in your life enlivens you. There is no limit to the quality to which you can elevate your experience of life. The space in your life must be larger, not smaller, to accommodate a teacher, especially a large teacher. When others criticize you for it, the space in your life must be large, not small, to accommodate that. This is an opportunity for you to become enlightened about having a teacher.

Chapter Two:
The Other Universe

The "other universe" is the Context out of which this universe came.

From time to time I will be using the term "the other universe," therefore, I want you to know what that means. Without going into logical proof, I want to give you a sense of the reality of the "unexistence" of another universe that allows this universe to be. The facts are that the universe we know has the appearance of existing in form, space, and time. The form it exists in is rarely questioned, except by certain scientists. The space it exists in is taken for granted, and the aspect of time is almost never questioned.

Now I want to ask you some questions. What right do you have to expect that the space in which this universe exists would itself exist? Secondly, given the space, what right do you have to expect that the form (matter) of the universe would exist within this space? Finally, given the foregoing, what right do you have to expect the universe to be changing, that is "time" passing? Very obviously we do not have the right to expect any of these and, nevertheless, it all is apparently happening.

What I really want to get behind is the question: what allows all of this to exist in space, form, and time? There has never been a universally satisfactory answer to this question. The fact that no suitable, universally acceptable answer has been generated over the ages indicates to me that there is no answer in the everyday terms that we conceive of answers.

173

Given our educational and cultural background, it is difficult to conceive a "nothing" as a "something." Nevertheless, Nothing as something is the only satisfactory answer there is, since everything else falls into the realm of disagreement and controversy. So the "other universe" is the Context out of which this universe came. It is that which allows this universe to be by *not* existing in space, form, and time. If it existed it would simply be more of this universe. In a sense, this universe is the "thought" of the other universe, perhaps not even a very profound thought, although we seem to think so based on the fact that we don't have anything else to compare it with.

Chapter Three:
Children As Contribution

Children bring a certain quality to life without which life would not be worth living.

Let's clarify something about children. They have a lot to teach us *and* they are a lot of trouble. Let's face it; they wet their pants, cry in public, demand to be fed, question our beliefs, spend our money, waste our time, and you can finish this very long list. Nevertheless, people continue to have children. There is clearly more to children than pain.

Children bring us something from the other universe for which we hunger as much as we hunger for food. They bring a certain quality to life without which life would not be worth living. If suddenly there were no children in the world, we would then know the contribution our children make to our lives. They are a fresh embodiment of the Self, immediately caught in a physical form. They have not had time to adopt the worldly beliefs that so structure and limit our lives. To a child, not only is everything possible, everything is.

Now, because they are also a lot of trouble, we often do not acknowledge the contribution our children bring to our lives. We blind ourselves to who our children really are: a new embodiment of God, the Context of the universe. God will never speak to you so clearly as through your child's laughter or tears. A child has not had time to forget how to experience life directly. Consequently, your children will know more than they are supposed to know. At times you will feel grossly ignorant in the presence of their knowing.

So, I want you to know what is primary and what is not primary. I want you to know which context works with children: pain or contribution. I want you to know which context holds the other, that is, which is senior and which is junior. Children are a magical contribution to our lives. Within this context of magical contribution is held that they are a pain and a lot of trouble. Therefore, acknowledge your children. Let them know what they contribute to your life. They know, but they don't know that you know, and they *want* to know that you know. It makes their lives worth living. Like you, they are here for the purpose of serving and being served by others, and they know it. Children make you a family. Without them, we are merely relationship. When they come into our lives we are family. Let them know that they make your life worthwhile. If you do, they will maintain their magical quality all of their lives and you will have them as friends in later years. If you don't, you endarken the world, for early in their lives children incorporate your thought, even your voice, into their minds. Don't burden the minds of your children with heavy, serious content.

Chapter Four:
The Voice-Over

*You sold out to your voice-over long ago and
now you think it's who you are.*

I want to alert you to a voice you are so identified with that
you think it is you. It is that voice in the back of your head which
is constantly telling you something. The something changes, but
the voice never does. You may be so unconsciously identified
with it that you don't know that it is there. You are probably
wondering, "What voice?" The voice that asks, "What voice?"
is the voice I am speaking of. Notice that when you pay attention you are listening to that voice. Please get the significance
of that statement: you are listening to that voice. The "you"
involved is the consciousness that you are, that you always have
been, and always will be.

However, there is a problem with "you." You probably sold
out to the voice-over many long years ago. You may have allowed
the voice-over to be who you are, or at least function as who you
are. If you did, the voice-over has been ordering you around
since then. In case you don't like that, there is only one thing to
do about it: come back. Inhabit your mind. Be here now.

If you are *very* unconscious about it, you are not even aware
that you have a voice-over. Nevertheless, having read this, you
will now begin to listen in. As you do, you will hear the most
incredible "stuff" you have ever heard. You will hear about
judgements and evaluations of other people. You will hear opinions, positions, beliefs, all the stuff that you allow to stand in the

way of your life, your work, and your relationships being all that they can be.

The voice-over was originally the internally parroted voice of a parent. Therefore your voice-over is likely to resemble a parental voice. On the other hand, it may sound like the opposite of the parental voice. Either position validates the origin of the voice from one or more parents. In the first case your mind went along with a parent's mind in order to get along and survive. In the second case your mind became compulsively contrary in order to survive. Either way you sold out and went away. Since then the voice-over has been running your life. You may have forgotten about the origin of the voice-over. In fact, you may have actively blocked out its origin. It doesn't matter. Either way, conscious or unconscious, you checked out and your mind has been running the show since then. Whether or not you are able to see the origin of the voice-over doesn't matter, for very soon it gained a life of its own and has been like a bull in a china shop since.

Again, the way to deal with the voice-over is to check back in and be responsible for being the consciousness that listens to the voice-over and then chooses to do whatever you do in life. In other words, doing what you do comes to have no relevance to what your mind tells you to do through your voice-over. The willingness to listen to the voice-over consciously and responsibly, and then to freely choose your life course, is the most advanced form of enlightenment you will ever know.

After sustained periods of doing this, the voice-over begins to quiet down a bit. Eventually, if you stay with it, the voice-over will become insignificant and may even disappear. As long as you simply follow orders from your voice-over, your life is nothing more than content-generated process. You are a stimulus-response machine. What a way to waste your life! Lighten up, life is a dream. Wake up!

Chapter Five:
Life As A Dream

*What happens when you become enlightened is
that you "wake up" in the dream of life.*

I want you to review your experience of dreams for a moment. A dream seems very real while it is in progress, doesn't it? Then you wake up and realize that "Wow! That was just a dream." In other words, the content of the dream evaporates. It disappears from your experience as if a gust of wind came along and blew it all away. You are left with "real life."

Now I want you to take a look at life. From where you are right now, let us say a miracle occurred and you could view the scene around you for three thousand years, without dying or growing old. What would happen to that scenario around you? The people would grow old, dry up, and blow away. The physical structures around you would crack, collapse and ultimately blow away in a gust of wind. Life is a dream on a slightly different time scale than your sleeping dreams. One day you will wake up and think something on the order of "Wow! That was just a dream."

Now, I want you to return to the arena of sleeping dreams for another insight. Perhaps you have had the experience of having the realization during a dream that it was a dream. I mean, you had the realization "Wow! This is just a dream" while you were dreaming. You may even have had the experience of gaining authorship of the dream while you were dreaming, so that you could actualize any content into the dream while the dream was in progress.

Now return to real life. What happens when you become enlightened is that you experience "waking up" during the dream of life, realizing that you are the author of it, and actualizing any content you choose to make real. However, like a sleeping dream, you can't actualize anything until you become conscious that life is a dream, while it is in progress. Someday you will wake up, at the moment of death, and realize that it was all a dream. Nevertheless, I prefer that you awaken now so that I can benefit from what you choose to make real in the world. You see, life is a "game" or a "dream" in which you are playing for now. If you know that, you can play responsibly, but not seriously, and move mountains if you choose. If you think this is "real life," you are essentially powerless to actualize your truth. Wake up and play!

Chapter Six:
Self As Other

The real illusion is that we are separate.

I want to express something here that can't be expressed. So, if you read this and get it, it will be because you already knew it in some way. What I want to express, or re-state, is that your actual identity in this world is everything except what you have been taught to believe that it is. As I told you before, relationship is that without which you cannot know that you are. You can only get this by doing the impossible: placing yourself in a lifeless world with no memory of life. In that condition you have absolutely no validation that you exist. You cannot look around and see other bodies and conclude that you are a body essentially similar to other bodies. You can see that you have some qualities in common with the rocks around you, namely, that you are physical. Therefore you may conclude that you are a rock, but it will never occur to you that you are a person. In fact, you won't even have a word like "person" or "human being." In fact, you won't have any words. Since there is no one to talk to, you will not develop language. So, relationship is that without which you cannot know you exist.

Since we live in a world of people, we assume that we are people, somewhat like other people. We look around us at our own bodies and we see arms, legs, trunk, genitals, chest, and so forth. We conclude that these body parts that are so close by must have something to do with who we are. Your body is the closest "thing" to where you think you are; therefore you think it must be you. This gives rise to a system of thinking and a language that supports this idea and you become "sure" that you "know" that you are your body. If you have an occasional thought to the contrary, you accuse yourself of thinking some bad craziness and you don't dare tell anyone you had such a thought. "Be real," you tell yourself. The part of your body that you assume that is most you is your face. Ironically, this is a part of your body that you can never see directly. You can see a reflection of it and people can tell you about it, but you can never see more than your nose and perhaps the tip of your tongue and some aspects of your lips.

Now, as you look out at the world you see who you really are and where you really are. You are who and where your consciousness is. Your consciousness is not "in here," it is "out there" where you perceive it. Nevertheless, the belief that you are "in here" is so strongly ingrained that most of us are able to deny who and where we really are. This denial has something to do with the fact that we deny, not only that we are "out there," but also that we have any responsibility for "out there." Notice if your beliefs are now saying "this guy is crazy."

The truth is that everything and nothing are the same and that we are both. You are not your body and your body is contained within you. You are everything which your consciousness creates, which is another way of saying "everything." You are everything. When you get unstuck from being your body only, you can look back and see that your body is part of you since it is contained in everything.

Now, since we are everything and since without each other we could not know that we exist, we are each other. Obviously, God became individual, many complete representations. So, when I know who I am, I am you, and you, and you, and so forth. From your standpoint, you are me, and him, and her, and so forth. This is the metaphysical model that allows us to take responsibility for ourselves, which is not separate from taking responsibility for the world itself. It involves giving up what psychoanalysts call "primary narcissism." Very few people give up all of their primary narcissism during their lives. What I am talking about here is giving up all of it. The purpose of giving it all up is to make your personal life work and to make the world work. These are not separate. If your world doesn't work, that is, if you are still stuck with the delusion of narcissism, then you have absolutely no chance of being all that you can be in terms of service to the world. Now, if you come at this issue of service from the position of sacrifice, that is not it. If you are "sacrificing" that the world might be served, you are still stuck being who you aren't. No one is served if you are at sacrifice. In fact, you actually subtract from the wellbeing of everyone you try to serve. On the other hand, if you come at this issue from the position of opportunity, the only thing that can happen is that the wellbeing of others (same as "you") is served, even when you seem to mishandle it.

In life, all of us begin from the condition that what we must do is "get." We must "get" to be good children, "get" to be smart teenagers, "get" to be mature adults. We must "get," or obtain, education, happiness, material goods that will further our survival and enhance our prestige. All of this "getting" is grounded in the universal desire for satisfaction. We live in an endarkened world, or, said another way, we live in a win or lose world wherein people do not generally win, or "get," unless someone else loses. Abundant evidence is available for this in the area of business, personal, and marital relationships where life is obviously a contest. There is a certain blindness involved in which few people seem to notice that "getting" doesn't bring satisfaction. Nevertheless, we find ourselves going back to it, back to it, and back to it in search of satisfaction, in the hope that the first few thousand times of "getting" were flukes and that the next "get" will finally bring the longed-for satisfaction. If only we could get that just-right sexual or marital partner, that adequate job, which has enough prestige attached or an adequately high salary, that terrific house, or that long-dreamed-of car that will make us complete and satisfied. We think that if we had only "gotten" the "right" parents or children, or if we only lived in that "right" part of the country, we would now be satisfied.

Now, the truth is that satisfaction is available for you right now without "getting" anything. The secret lies in giving, not getting. However, there is a catch to this: if you give, that is serve others, in order to "get," that is not service, it is simply more "getting" designed to look like giving and it doesn't work any better than straight "getting." To arrive at true satisfaction in life, you must give up "getting" *and* "giving to get," which is the same thing. In other words, to be in satisfaction you must give up what you ordinarily think of as "you," and become who you really are, your actual Self. In thus surrendering you will come to grips with the fact that the way you have run your life hasn't been working, regardless of how well you may have the "symbols" together to prove that it works. Most of us are strongly attached to our symbols and the thought of giving them up is very threatening. By giving them up, I don't mean not having them; I mean transforming them so that they are not "yours," but belong to others and are used in the service of others. Giving yourself away, or surrendering, doesn't mean becoming poor, necessarily. Surrendering to your life *does* mean giving up the importance of all those things you have been "getting" and admitting that the game of life is over and you won, even though the "proof" is not at hand. When you do this, you will notice that you are satisfied and nurtured by whatever relationship you are in. You will have joy in whatever job you do and wherever you live will be the place that is satisfying for you. You will not have to have the perfect lover, spouse, home, car, location, parents, children, for by giving yourself away you are outside the win/lose system and you have won it all. Your idiotic "pictures" about the way it all "should" be will fade and drop away, and you won't be stuck thinking that you or others are better or worse than anyone else. Your ability to love will be an actualized fact. Oddly enough, when you give up "getting," it usually happens that the environment around you begins to give you all those things you thought you wanted, but it doesn't really matter since your life is not about "getting," but about giving or serving. I say that you can't deny who you are any longer, and that who you are is, in fact, about giving.

Chapter Seven:
The Story

*You are not the product of your environment as
your story would have it.*

As people progress through life, in the ordinary course of
events, they collect a memory of what happened on the journey.
As time passes these memories are reworked and edited, practiced and preached, until they come into line with a false identity
supported by a "story." The purpose of the story is three-fold: (1)
to make the teller right and others wrong, (2) to explain the
reasons things turned out the way they did, and (3) to give the
teller a sense of who he is, which, without the story, is *apparently*
missing.

Oddly enough, it fails on all three counts, but persists in the
mind for the sake of allaying anxiety. Inevitably the story does
not come out consistent with the truth of what happened. It
tends to come out more like what the teller would like to have
happened, what he thinks should have happened. In the process, memories can actually be reworked and changed. In
psychoanalysis this is known as a "screened memory." In truth,
all of us carry screened memories, in some form, although we are
the last to become conscious about it. So, if anything, the story
makes you wrong because of its gross inaccuracies.

On the second count, the story more or less succeeds, but not
really. It does provide the teller a certain degree of reasonableness about the "why" of how things turned out. However, the
answers to "Why?" never provide mastery about how things are

turning out now. So, reasonableness is synonymous with uselessness, and in this sense the story is a total failure.

The third factor, identity, is quite deceptive. It really looks as though we should be our mother's children, products of the schools we went to, the sum total of our beliefs, positions, opinions, tastes, and so forth. And yet, this sort of identity comes so quickly and is so quickly gone. It leaves one with a certain lack of satisfaction about "Who am I?" Not to mention the fact that human beings generate, with regularity, creations that simply cannot be explained on the basis of previous experience.

I suggest to you that you are not the product of your environment, as your story would have it. I suggest to you that your story does not make you right, except at great expense to your own aliveness. I suggest to you that your story in no way explains things in a way that provides you with mastery of your life. Most significantly, I suggest to you that you are the consciousness that indwells the mind which has collected this story and, as such, the last thing you need a story for is to identify who you are. Becoming enlightened has a lot to do with giving up the "importance" of your story on all three counts and, ultimately, giving up your story altogether. Only when you have given up the "importance" of your story can you begin to have a significant impact on the world. Your story prevents you from serving the world and sticks you reciting mind stuff for the rest of your days.

Chapter Eight:
That Which Runs The World

*You happen to be the carrier of the most power-
ful instrument known in the universe.*

You know, it really looks as if people run the world, doesn't
it? I mean it seems that a president runs the executive branch of
the government, that dictators call the shots in their realms,
coaches call the plays on the field of sport, and so forth. But, ask
yourself, do they really? And, if they do, out of what do they
make their decisions?

On the other hand, it appears that organizations, institutions, and governments actually are the controlling factors. They
control the flow of money and seemingly make the big decisions
that have a profound effect on many lives. But, ask yourself, is
there anything more fundamental that we could identify that
runs presidents, dictators, coaches, organizations, institutions,
and governments? Is there something common to all of these that
calls the shots for them all and uses them merely as the vehicle
through which to express itself? If you could identify something
more fundamental that underlies all of these, would you not then
have the power to run presidents, institutions, etc.?

Puzzle over this a moment. I want you to really get the sense
that you operate in a world of illusion, that you don't actually
know what runs your world and the world, unless of course, you
know the answer. I want you to know that none of the above are
the right answer. None of the above come close to running the
world. The correct answer was known to the likes of Christ, Karl

Marx, and Thomas Jefferson, to name a few. What did these three people know about the way the world operates that you don't, that, if you knew, you could begin to exercise your potential power in the world?

What these people knew is that ideas run the world. People and institutions do not run the world, ideas do. Ah! There is a problem with this, isn't there? People who generate ideas aren't glorified. People who *implement* ideas are glorified in the world of agreement. Now I want to tell you the ultimate secret: people who generate ideas don't run the world either, ideas themselves do. People who generate ideas, then, are merely the physical form through which ideas are expressed into the world. Ideas are not physical. That which runs the world, therefore, is not physical. Only when you give up, not only the quest for glory, but also the quest for a physical embodiment of that which runs the world, can you experience your power in the world. People spend lifetimes chasing illusions.

To express an idea into the world requires that it have a physical place in which to dwell. It just so happens that the individual is the only dwelling place for an idea. So if you become conscious of an idea you want to express into the world, you must give it the form and intention required so that it will gain access to the only place an idea can dwell: within individuals. Once an idea gains adequate access to individuals, the only thing that can happen is that it will express itself in the physical universe. Nothing is, except that thinking makes it so. When enough people become carriers of an idea, a process begins which leads inexorably to the expression of the idea. There is nothing that is not possible to an idea whose time has come, that is, an idea that gains adequate numbers of individuals in which to dwell. Democratic government, spiritual movement, women's suffrage, man on the moon, end of starvation, war, crime, all of these are accomplished or accomplishable. But every idea looks impossible until it is done; then, of course it was possible.

I want you to begin to get a sense of your power. You are the carrier of the most powerful instrument known in the universe: an idea. You can express those ideas into reality to the degree that you clear your mind of opinion, position, judgement, and thus become enlightened. The enemies to ideas are these very mind structures which I just named. Thus it is that you block expression of your power in this world. And you do it, no one does it to you. Your ability and willingness to hold an idea is the most accurate measure of enlightenment there is in this world. When you are able and willing to hold ideas, you can also become the conduit through which ideas flow. But only if you are willing to give up the thought that you are somehow more important because ideas seem to come from you. They do not come *from* you, they come *through* you. For ideas to come through you, you must clear your mind of "stuff."

Chapter Nine:
Up Against The Wall

Doing "something" gets you to the wall, doing "nothing" get you through.

I want to make a few comments about the situation you encounter when you have done all that you know to do to become enlightened and still you are in a condition of endarkenment or heaviness. I call this being "up against the wall." You are up against the wall only when you take responsibility for all of your experience in life. Be careful in reading this to be certain that you are truly up against the wall, that is, that you have taken responsibility for all of your experience. After looking at that for a while, if you see that you are, in fact, in a condition of responsibility for all of your experience, I want you to know what will get you to the other side of the wall where the experience of satisfaction and mastery of life is. Nothing will get you through the wall. I mean that both ways. First nothing you can do will ever get you through that wall. The way you got up to the wall is that you "did" all there was to do. Therefore, by definition, there is no more that you can do. Second, only Nothing (Context) will get you through the wall. What that means is that getting through the wall is a miracle. It is a miracle that there even is the "other side" of the wall. Now, I want you to know when it will happen: when it happens. Like an earthquake or a flash of lightning, it will happen when it happens. You can't "make" it happen. Next I want you to know how long it will take when it happens: no time. You will simply be on the other side. You will have no memory of going through because it didn't happen in time. It happens outside of time, like all experience and all miracles.

Since this miracle happens only when you are truly up against the wall, your job is to stay up against it. This is not a place the mind likes to be. The mind will do anything to avoid that wall. So you must be bigger than your mind to stay in the experience of responsibility for your life. If even a small part of your experience becomes unstuck, you have no chance of passing through the wall to satisfaction and enlightenment.

After the miracle occurs you will find that you will not stay on the other side of the wall. You will vacillate back and forth. While this is happening, you will have more opportunities to recreate your condition of responsibility that is the only path to enlightenment. When you are up against the wall again, there will be a shift in your experience of it. The desperation will go out of it. You will be on the other side about being on this side. That is, you will be enlightened about being in the dark again. You will spend a good portion of your life shifting back and forth.

When you finally settle on the enlightened side of the wall, if you do, there will be another shift in your experience. Not only will you be responsible and enlightened, you will also have mastery over it. With this mastery will come into being the ability to create in your life. Before mastery, you can only create what is. After mastery, you can choose whatever you want, to be. That is, you can bring into being and cause to disappear from being any contexts you choose. You will then know your Self as the cause of all contexts. You have always been the cause of contexts; however, now you will experience it. After the experience you will be able to look back into the "past" and see and experience your Self as the source of it all, even when you were sure you were not. In the present you may source contexts such as wellbeing, health, satisfaction, education, vocation, influenza, parent, child, communication, and so forth. For example, if you source yourself as the context of wellbeing, you will bring to whatever situation or relationship system you happen to be involved in the quality of wellbeing. Up to this point in life you have probably discovered yourself as the context of several qualities, and what you have missed out on is the discovery of yourself as the Context that generated those contexts.

You have probably been somewhat puzzled, if you noticed at all, that you embodied the quality of whatever context you discovered yourself as being.

I want to return, for a moment, to that stage in your progression toward permanent enlightenment when you were up against the wall. At that time you had done everything there was to do to become responsible for your experience of life, and the payoff simply wasn't there; that is, enlightenment was simply not at hand. The way we ordinarily talk about that point in the progression toward mastery is called "boring." The qualities of fatigue and lethargy are present and pervasive in your experience of life. People find it extremely difficult to stay with boredom and create the experience of being responsible for that also. What usually happens is that you drum up some drama in your life: you leave someone, you pick a fight, you quit your job, you spend more money than you have, or do something that you know will not work. It becomes very clear that you are not master of your life, but at least it isn't boring anymore. What I am telling you is that boredom is the last stage through which you must pass before you miraculously go through the wall. To the degree that you avoid boredom, you will never make it through the wall.

Most of us will experience boredom in the contexts of work or relationship. You know what to do when you are bored with your work or your relationship. You either make trouble or you leave. Doing either one of these, however, requires justification, so you engage in a process, a content-determined process, the purpose of which is to justify leaving or making trouble in your work or your relationship. If you are capable of swift, sure make-wrongs of other people, it won't take you long to have your justifications together. After you have done whatever you have justified, you will have a story to tell others when it comes to the fact that you made trouble and/or left. I repeat that this is a content-determined process. The content is your mind patterns. You have checked out, are no longer participating, and refuse to be responsible. You, as cause of contexts, are not there and your content (mind) is running you. If you are awake and witnessing it all, it looks very confusing to you. When you finish this content-determined process, you will then still be faced with the problem of transforming your life into a Context-determined process. In other words, your problem will be to get back to being up against the wall again. When you do, boredom will always come up just before you go through the wall to mastery of your life.

Chapter Ten:
Where The Mess Is

Enlightenment is not a way to avoid the mess the world is in, but is itself the only responsible confrontation of it.

When it comes to the issue of becoming enlightened there is an illusion which presents itself almost every time. The illusion is called "the easy way out." Enlightenment looks like an easy way out. It looks as though we can leave the mess the world is in and go for cosmic enlightenment. In the process we can leave family and friends, who don't seem to understand this enlightenment stuff, stuck in the mess they helped us make. So, the apparency is that the mess comes to be behind us, "back there" or "in the past" or "back there with them." When you try to live with that, you must confront the paradoxical duality of perfection/mess that is the very substance of enlightenment. On the one hand the world is perfect. This perfection includes the suffering that is going on with such great intensity. It also includes the fact that the suffering is self-induced by humanity and that it appears that some people are imposing suffering on other people. The universe is in a perfect dance. On the other hand, we are in a terrible mess, and we must do something about it. If you go for the real article of enlightenment, you must contain this duality and not become stuck at either end of it. At one and the same time, you must realize that it is perfect and we are in a large mess. If you get stuck in the fact that it is perfect, you cannot make any sort of contribution to handling the mess. We will call

194

you narcissistic, but not enlightened. If you become stuck in the fact that it is a mess, you are at the effect of it; you become part of the mess. When you are the mess, you cannot have a powerful impact on handling the mess. Your life-long occupation becomes suffering.

So, when you go for outer space enlightenment it looks as though you are leaving the mess behind, and what you find out is that the mess is always and forever directly in front of you. Too bad. You get to be enlightened while you confront the mess. When you stay with it you find out that you created the mess, the mess your perceptions and your mind tell you is there. You made it by virtue of what you did *and* what you didn't do. And you don't get to blame anyone else. If you blame someone else, you become part of the mess with no chance of handling it. The veil of suffering becomes too much and you become too little. In effect, you become part of the mess and simply suffer. Therefore, when you become enlightened you are not the mess and the mess is not behind you, rather you created the mess and the mess is directly in front of you. This condition gives you the opportunity to go for it and change it. You can rework it, mold it, open up the space for the world to work in a very real way.

When you are enlightened you discover yourself as the context of wellbeing. You can only discover yourself as this context because you are, yourself, a well Being. So, enlightenment is a recontextualization of the experience of your life so that what was a suffering mess prior to enlightenment becomes nurturing experience after enlightenment and in fact a magnificent opportunity to express your Self. When this happens you are, indeed, a well Being and a well Being is powerful.

Now, it is not enough to discover yourself as the context of wellbeing. You must then beat the content of life into shape. You can only do that from the context of wellbeing. From any other context you do not have adequate power. So what was content-generated process before enlightenment becomes Context-generated process after enlightenment. The content of your life recognizes its master: Context. Prior to that event you are stuck in being the effect of the content in life. Stimulus-response-stimulus-response-stimulus-response- . . . Each response is a new stimulus which gives rise to another response, so that it actually becomes response-response-response-response- . . . When you discover yourself as the Context of life, you can interrupt this at any point you choose. You can generate any sort of context you choose at any time you choose. You can cause any context you choose to disappear whenever you like. When you materialize the context of wellbeing, you have the power to absolutely beat the content of life into shape. You can take responsibility for the mess the world is in without sacrificing your sanity. It becomes an opportunity (which is nothing more or less than a transformed burden). Now, the mess is truly in front of you and you wouldn't want it any other way. It is the perfect place for the mess to be. The mess is perfect, especially at the interface with an endarkened world.

Chapter Eleven:
At The Interface

It is exactly there, where the world makes you wrong for your enlightenment, that your opportunity exists to cause the world to work; if you are comfortable, that's not it.

When the time comes in your life to become enlightened you will find that what you want to do is take your enlightenment and manifest it in this physical universe. You will want to transform it into a contribution to others, for this is the nature of true enlightenment. If you prefer to keep it to yourself, you haven't gotten the real article.

By being enlightened and saying so, you are also, necessarily, endarkened. People who are totally enlightened do not know that there is any other state of being. They simply live in a state of grace and for them everyone is enlightened. If you can see that some people are not enlightened, that means that you carry some darkness within you. Only in that way can you see any contrast in the world that informs you that there are different conditions. So the sequence for you is enlightened, endarkened, enlightened, endarkened, enlightened, endarkened, and so on. You blink on and off. And that's OK. Actually, since that is your condition, it had better be OK.

Now, since you are enlightened, you will want to do something with it, and this is where the problem is. When you carry your light into a dark world, that world will make you wrong, very wrong. However, most of what you perceive as make-wrongs will be the reactivation of your own endarkenment. You then have the opportunity to separate what is your own reactivated self-criticism from what is out there which definitely decreases the quality of the experience of life for you and for others. This separation process will probably consume several years of your life. When you are totally centered, you will then see that there is, in fact, some very heavy darkness out there.

The problem, which is actually an opportunity, occurs at the interface between the light and the dark. It is exactly there, where your greatest discomfort is, that your opportunity exists to enlighten the world and the people in it. So, if you are always comfortable, you aren't contributing anything. The form this takes is highly variable. The people you work with may find your new-found inner and outer enthusiasm difficult to tolerate. People who live in darkness hate enlightened people with great intensity. This hate, and the acts that are done out of it, are an opportunity for you to express your Self in the world. And it hurts. Too bad. Perhaps your spouse, lover, or co-worker will reject you. As the space you exist in expands, you may well outgrow the size of the space in which you are held by your relationships. They may prefer to make you wrong and reject you rather than expand to accommodate your new size. One thing is certain: one of these two things will happen: you will be rejected or they will expand. If you are rejected, chances are slim that it will be in an honest and open manner. Probably you will be criticized and blamed and then turned away. The justifications that cover this process are elaborate and, if done by an artistic person, sound very reasonable. The endarkened rejector must tell lies that he or she can also believe. So it hurts. Your enlightenment brings you pain. Too bad. It is exactly in that interface of pain that you have an opportunity to make a difference in the world. If you literally outsize your job or relationship, you then have the opportunity to go on to something and/or someone that will actually make a contribution to the quality of life on our planet.

So enlightenment is not all fun and games. If you think you are becoming enlightened to have fun, think twice. Be certain that you want to expand, for it may mean giving up something or someone. When that happens your choice is to hold what happens as a disaster or an opportunity. If you hold it as an opportunity your new-found largeness will be a space from which you can expand again if you choose. <u>You will never get so large that you can't expand some more.</u> <u>In retrospect, looking back, have compassion on those whom you left behind. Their time simply had not come yet.</u> They had no sense of choice about what they did with you. You don't have to exclude them as worthless human beings. People become enlightened when their time comes and not before. So, treat them with decency, especially if they rejected you. When you become a context large enough to contain those who oppose and reject you, your life is suddenly illuminated.

Chapter Twelve:
The Creation Of Context

Context makes the direct experience of life available to you by re-absorbing all that you have disowned in life.

Context is that condition within the Self in which all of your positionality can dwell. It makes the direct experience of life available to you again by re-absorbing all that you have disowned in life.

In the ordinary course of events, as your mind grows older, it selects certain positions to be right about. This process necessarily forces you to disown a significant part of your direct experience of life, namely, those parts that are made wrong by your positions. The creation of context is a reversal of this process. Only by seeing your positions as mere positions can you discover context. While you think your positions are the truth, you can never discover or recreate your own context. You were born with context as a free gift. Most of what you have been up to since then has been in the service of building a mind prison through the adoption of positions. In your relationships, your positions mechanically produce opposing positions in others. So, you have a very accurate index of when one of your positions is reactivated: people around you begin to become positional and they oppose you. When your relationships are not running smoothly you can always trace it to reactivated positions. Until you see that, you are sentenced to the prison of your mind.

Within your mind you will notice that there is conflict and suffering from time to time. This is the intrapsychic result of positionality. You see, your mind adopts positions that make each other wrong. While you are identified with your mind you will have to experience your Self as the suffering entity, that is, the entity that is in conflict. After you separate your identity from your mind, you will have the experience that there is some suffering going on in your general vicinity, but it will become somewhat irrelevant. Having the suffering of your mind be irrelevant is an interesting spot to be in. There are a lot of enlightened people who are there and convinced that there isn't much more to do about it. Somehow God must have meant it to be this way. It is just the "karma." I want you to know that it doesn't have to be that way. Cleaning it up completely means recreating context within your Self. This is accomplished by becoming conscious of your positions, then including them within you as positions instead of truth. A context, then, is a structure that can contain all of the positions, including those positions that make the context wrong. In fact, those are the most important positions to include. Unless they are included you do not have context, you have another position.

If you want to create the experience of yourself as the cause of all contexts, you must deal with all the smaller contexts. This is another way of saying that you will not experience your Self as the creator of your universe until you have recontextualized all of your experience. When you deal with all of your smaller contexts you can find out the truth that when you discover yourself, you are the Context from which all contexts flow.

Chapter Thirteen:
Context As Sanity

A context is a structure that contains all positions, including those that seem conflicting, in such a way that they support each other.

This word "context," as I use it here, is difficult to get a handle on. Just when you think you have got it, you find out that you don't have it at all. So, I want to talk about it directly as it relates to sanity. I am not talking about the "sanity" that is a function of agreement, that is, when people tell you you are sane. I am talking about that experience you have from time to time (I hope) that your mind, even *your* mind, is totally together. You are in the experience that you cause your own experience, all of it, and that it is perfect. I call this the creation of context within the mind. Only the Self can create context, but the context for sanity is created by the Self *within the mind*. The context that causes sanity is one that transforms insanity, that is, the constant internal opposition of positions within the mind, into sanity. Conflicting positions still exist within the mind, but after the context for sanity is created they are held in such a way that they nurture you and support you rather than tear you down.

A context, therefore, is a structure that contains all positions, including those that seem conflicting, in such a way that they support each other. A complete context (actually there are no incomplete contexts) is one that actually contains its own opposition. So, in the case of the context for sanity, for example, the fact of insanity is contained within this context. Therefore,

202

when insanity comes up, which is the condition of no responsibility for one's own experience and positional opposition within
the mind, it is held within the context of sanity. Within that
context even insanity contributes to sanity.

Now, the principles that run your mind are not different
from those that run your interpersonal life, organizations,
nations, and the world at large. At the interpersonal level you can
create a context for friendship, for example. Within this context
even unfriendly thoughts and actions are held and contribute to
the friendship. There is an equivalent context for lovers. At the
organizational level, the context for the realization of the purpose
of the organization is created. Within this context are contained
all possible positions about how the purpose of the organization
should be achieved, including the position that it can't be done.
If your organization is achieving its purpose, take a look and you
will see that such a context is in fact already created. National
purpose is realized in the same way. As yet, little in the way of
world contexts has been created. However, I regard the Hunger
Project as the first real world context. The Hunger Project has as
its purpose the creation of the context for the end of hunger and
starvation by 1997. Within this context all positions about how
this can/should be done are held, including the very opposition
to the idea of doing it. I regard the Hunger Project as the first
instance of creation of a context for sanity at a world level and I
expect more to follow.

So context is a sort of framework in which all positions are
held. Context causes sanity at all levels: interpersonal, organizational, national, and world. Create contexts in your life and
watch your life work. Don't bother, and watch your life be
content-generated process: stimulus–response–stimulus–response–stimulus–response– . . . When context is created it
grinds up content into a Context-generated process. Ultimately,
you are the generator of all contexts, for this is the power that
the individual has: to create all contexts. This is the way you
run your life and life, in general, around you. Individuals are
powerful in this regard.

I want you to notice that word: "individual." It means,
literally "undividable two." I suggest to you that the two that are
undividable, while you live in a body, are mind and Self or, said

another way, content and Context. Content is insane. Context makes even content sane and consistent with purpose by containing the truth as paradox.

Chapter Fourteen:
The Truth As Paradox

The truth is never a position you believe in, nor
is it the opposing position you don't believe in; the
truth is the context in which beliefs are held.

I want to give you a glimpse of that which can't really be
talked about: the nature of truth and the Self. You must remember that language was not designed to express the truth. In
ordinary, everyday life, what people mean by the term "truth" is
a position they believe in. This sort of "truth" mechanically gives
rise to an opposite opposing position, so when you say "X" is
right, that gives rise to the opposing position that "not-X" is
right, with absolute reliability. It doesn't happen just sometimes; it happens each and every time you take a position. A
position always calls into being its own opposition. This should
give you a hint about what the truth is.

The truth, with respect to "X" and "not-X," is that "X" and
"not-X" are both right and they are both wrong. The truth, then
is a context that contains the paradox of opposite position both
being right and both being wrong. It happens that the mind is
not capable of holding the truth as paradox. Therefore you cannot experience the truth with your mind, which is a right/wrong
machine designed for survival of individuality.

This all comes into clear focus in the realm of love and
commitment. When you say "I love you" to someone, that automatically creates its opposite which may be "I don't love you"
or "I hate you." As you can see, there is sometimes more than

one opposite. So, if you are the carrier of "I love you" and you put it out as a position, it mechanically produces its opposite somewhere. That somewhere may be in the mind of the person you love from a position. What may come up in her mind is, "But I don't love you." In case they come up with the same position, "I love you," then you will become the carrier of "I don't love you." "I love you / I don't love you" is known as ambivalence. The only way you can avoid ambivalence is if the "love object" is willing to carry "But I don't love you." If both of you take the position "I love you," what will happen is that you both become the carriers of the opposing position. This inevitable condition of ambivalence calls into being commitment, if there is intention for the relationship to last. A relationship of "I love you / I don't love you" can only be contained in your Self, the context of love. If your fundamental context is love, then "I love you / I don't love you" can be held in that context and both positions contribute to the context. The outcome is that "I don't love you" is a validation of the context of love in which it is held and powers the relationship. Creating a context of love, that is, being your Self, or the Self, means a willingness to put your very existence on the line in the form of commitment. You must see that love cannot be maintained, has never been maintained, will never be maintained, from the level of the mind.

Likewise, commitment cannot be created at mind level. At the level of the mind commitment becomes a concept, not an experience. The concept "I am committed to you" is a position and mechanically creates its own opposition somewhere, either in your mind or the mind of your partner. In this way it is handled by the mind in the same way "I love you" is handled. Therefore, "I am committed to you" must be created from the Self, that is, it is an experience. The experience of creation of commitment occurs outside of time and, as such, can only be reported upon. This means in practical terms that you simply look to see if the commitment is created, and then tell the truth about it. You can't make yourself, or your partner, create a commitment.

Here is what you *can* do about it: develop the intention to have your relationship work. Out of your intention, in the condition of integrity, comes a naturally created commitment. It is simply there, not as a concept, but as a natural, living, spontaneous commitment. Obviously then, integrity and intention are the qualities you must uncover in your Self if you want relationships that work.

So, here is how to accomplish it all. Life works perfectly if you simply do what is appropriate with the fundamentals of intention and integrity. What is appropriate to this fundamental level is: (1) tell the truth, all of it, at all times, and (2) be absolutely true to your ideals until you realize that your ideals are actually your blocks in life. At that point they will become your former ideals. After that, you simply do what works. Fundamentally, what works is to tell the truth, all of it, at all times. This brings you back to the truth as paradox. The truth is that "I love you / I don't love you" and "I am committed to you / I am not committed to you" exist at all times, side by side, in the same space of the Self. If you really get this at the level of unity of being, it becomes unimportant who is carrying which position at any given moment. The Self is the only context large enough to contain a working love relationship between two people.

The path to the Self is communication. If you have no intention of your relationship working you will avoid communication. When and if you get beyond avoidance of communication, you will have to confront the truth as paradox. Your positional mind won't like it that you also contain the opposite position. Nevertheless, the truth *is* paradox and only the truth works. To get the truth as paradox, you have to check back into your life and be your Self.

Chapter Fifteen:
Checking Out

When you check out of a relationship, that is quit participating, you may actually stick around physically. However the relationship dies for the want of your presence, and the way that you know you quit participating is that the relationship becomes very dramatic as the other person tries to recall you to participation.

I want to remind you of that relationship you left, the one you thought had so much potential, the one in which you became disappointed and disillusioned with the other person. You know the one I mean. I want to let you know what really happened there. I don't mean to explain the reasons it didn't work out, you have already done that. Looking back on it, it is perfectly obvious to you why things happened the way they did. Obviously the other person let you down, wasn't strong enough, needed you too much or some such "reasons." I know that you have it all figured out in retrospect. So, I'm not interested in going over that stuff with you. I want to let you know what really happened, not reinforce your posthumous rationalizations.

What really happened was that at some point in the linear progression of the relationship you checked out. I am not referring to the time you actually left; that came much later or perhaps hasn't come yet. I am referring to the time you quit participating in the relationship. Your body/mind machine stuck around, but you checked out and quit participating; that is, you, your Self, left. So, what happened was that you became the non-participant observer of the relationship between your mind/body machine and the other Self. Now, you didn't acknowledge what you did and you lied about it, to the other Self and to yourself. Nevertheless, everyone involved knew what had happened. Then the other Self began to try to retrieve you and cause you to participate again. When this happened, you made them very wrong, perhaps out loud or perhaps only to yourself. At that point you began to collect reasons to leave the other person. When you made him adequately wrong to assuage your guilty conscience, you announced that you were leaving and left, or perhaps you just left, via the back door. Whichever way out you selected, it still bothers you. You know, underneath all the reasons, what you did. You know that you made it turn out the way that it did and didn't. You also know that it had nothing to do with all that stuff that happened after you checked out and denied the other Self your Being. You know that all that happened after you checked out was a direct result of having checked out. You also know that you have it all rationalized in a very reasonable manner that gives you no mastery, only explanations. You know about all those short-comings you saw in the other person, don't you? Guess whose short-comings those really are? Right! Whatever you can't admire and respect in another is something you have within you which you are too small to admit to having. That's just the way it is. Too bad.

I want to let you know also about what will give you mastery in your relationships. Don't check out. If you do, clearly acknowledge that as what you did. Do not, I repeat, do not, make the other person wrong for the reaction he or she has to your having checked out. If you are powerful enough to check out, you are also powerful enough to check back in. However, when you do, you will have to confront the stonewall of reasons you made up to explain everything retrospectively. That is the price you pay to get the opportunity to give up being right. You will do well, if you want relationships that work in your life, to check back in at your earliest convenience and get off being right.

Checking out appears rather infantile when you drop the rationalizations about it. Actually, the only thing an infant can do to dominate and manipulate is check out and not participate.

Giving up your checking out and leaving patterns means leaving those infantile activities to infants. Presumably you are beyond that now.

In case this has been a pattern for you, and it probably has, you can do yourself a favor by cleaning up your act. What this means is to communicate to that string of people behind you that you are off your position about how wrong they were and also that you know that you checked out. This will complete those relationships for you, and you can experience yourself as the whole, complete person you are. Until then, the price you pay is a life of content-generated process. That is all it can be when you have checked out and not acknowledged responsibility for it.

Chapter Sixteen:
Backing Up Through Life

Those who have checked out of their lives, who are not participating, must of necessity "back up" through life in order to avoid the experience of responsibility for the messes they make.

I want you to imagine a person backing up, perhaps you, all the while busily explaining to everyone around exactly where he has been. From time to time this person trips and falls or simply runs over someone else. As soon as the pieces are put together, this person says something to the effect of, "Gee, I'm sorry I fell down and ran over you, but as you see, it is quite understandable." Then, looking backwards, he continues, "It appears that I took a right turn and then a left; then I tripped over this block here and there you were in the way just as I fell. You know you really can't blame me because, as you can see, I have been looking backwards, besides which, as I told you, it's all perfectly obvious what happened." Perhaps you would marvel at such a fool and become incredulous at the logic he uses. Nevertheless, this is exactly how most of us go through life.

The person who backs up through life is operating at the effect of his own mind and the circumstances and conditions of life, in other words, the content of life. He has a billiard ball theory of reality. Everything is perfectly obvious in retrospect. The explainability of it all serves him as an excuse for his gross condition of no responsibility. If you encounter one of these individuals, you are in for some trouble, all of which is perfectly explainable and reasonable, however. Nevertheless, after you are run down by this irresponsible clutz, the fact that it all makes such good sense in retrospect is of little consolation to you.

To put this in words you will have a hard time understanding, you are dealing with a person engaged in a content-determined process. This is made possible by the fact that the person has checked out, has no integrity at an operating level, and has no overall purpose in life. In short, there is no Context for such a life. You have a stimulus-response machine to deal with. In case you are the person backing up through life, I want you to know what to do about it.

Turn around. Check back into your life. Start participating. Quit using your reasonableness to explain why you run over others and dent yourself from time to time. Get in touch with your own natural integrity. Keep your agreements. Tell the truth. Make room for commitment in your life. In other words, become that which you always have been: the Context of your life. Make your life a Context-determined process.

As long as your life content is the context in which it is held, it will not move forward except at the expense of others and yourself. There will be one tragedy after another in your life. That is the nature of a content-determined life. The first thing for you to do is to start to acknowledge responsibility for the messes you make in life and quit laying them at the doorsteps of others. Then, I suggest that you get a purpose around which your life can come to make some sense. Select something you consider worth your attention and go all out for it. This something will yield the most satisfaction if you experience it as a contribution to others. After you have turned around, it all becomes a very natural process. A Contextualized life can only work out.

Chapter Seventeen:
A Master Practicing Or
Practicing To Be A Master?

*Perhaps you have wondered how people come
to experience themselves as "master" in their lives.
The answer is simple: they consider it to be so true
that no proof is required.*

I am going to describe two modes of experiencing life and
then tell you the most fundamental determinant relating to
which mode you happen to be in. The first one is that of practicing to be a master, although you probably call it by some other set
of words. Nevertheless, you will recognize the description. The
events of life are organized into a pattern of struggling for mastery without completion of the experience of your mastery. Your
experience resembles the age-old riddle of trying to reach a wall
by successively taking half the distance to the wall with each
step. No matter how close you come to the wall, you never reach
it. There is always an infinite number of steps left to reach the
wall. In the experience of your life, likewise, there seem to be an
infinite number of steps left until you reach the condition of
master of the experience of your life. It is always just beyond:
with that just right job, that just so relationship, those perfect
friends whom you haven't met yet, that new car you think will
complete your experience of mastery. Yet, as each new circumstance is completed, you notice that the experience of satisfaction
isn't quite all there. Something is missing and you can't quite put
your finger on it. No matter what you do, that's not it.

The other mode of experiencing life is that of master. Exactly the same conditions and events prevail; however, it is all incorporated into the mode of a master practicing life. Difficult situations still befall you; however, they become a contribution to your enrichment. At all times you feel whole and complete, and everything that happens in your life validates your wholeness and your completeness. This experience extends to your relationships as well. Your spouse or parent may express hostility and rejection toward you and you take that into your experience in such a way that it validates the worth of the other person as well as your own worth. Or, if they are not communicative, that is taken into your experience in such a way that the silence is exactly the contribution that is appropriate in the relationship. You are master of life and all that comes by for your experience validates, confirms, and contributes to your context as master. Whether things are "good or bad" by the standards of the world is quite irrelevant.

So, we have before us two modes of experiencing life; (1) practicing to be a master, and (2) a master practicing. I can't stress to you too much that external events do not determine which mode you are in. Anyone in their right mind would choose number 2, wouldn't they? Evidently not, for it is the purest choice there is in life and yet, what we see in the world is people practicing to be masters and never quite making it. This brings us to the issue of the fundamental determinant of which mode you happen to be in. Like all true statements it is utter simplicity: YOU SAY SO. If you feel stuck in practicing to be a master and never quite making it, ask yourself: Why don't I say so?

In the moment that you say so, it is so. I must tell you that the content of your life is not what changes when you say "I am a master practicing." What changes when you say that is that everything and everyone in your life is transformed in your experience and it all becomes a contribution to your practice of mastery. You don't have to wait until you are on your death bed to become a master practicing. You can become a master practicing from where you are right now. Simply say so. Then, consciously take every event in your life as a demonstration of your mastery.

Chapter Eighteen:
Transformation Of Relationships
By A Master Practicing

When you experience yourself as the "master"
in your life, you will find that you can instantly and
magically transform the quality of any relationship
by simple consideration.

There are certain advantages to being a master practicing. For one thing, your relationships are transformed. So, if you have been putting up with, or trying to change, your mother and simply being frustrated, all that is transformed. I don't mean that your mother will become enlightened and start treating you like a prince or a princess. No! A master of life has no need for a mother who acts the way she is "supposed to." In fact, your mother's craziness (if she is nuts) becomes more grist for your mastery mill. The crazier she acts, the more mastery you have. If you look at her and get a large pain in your stomach, the pain in your stomach becomes more contributing material to your mastery. Why? Because you say so. No other reason. If that is not your experience, then you didn't say so. On the other hand, if your mother becomes enlightened (and she might), then her enlightenment is a validation of your mastery. Why? Because you say so. For no other reason.

You see, a master practicing lets life be the way it is. When you let life be the way it is, you will find out that it validates and supports you. Always. So, if life is not validating and supporting you, you are not letting it be the way it is. At that point, when you are willing to let it be the way it is, a certain satisfaction comes over you. Said another way, you create the context of satisfaction by doing nothing. From the context of satisfaction you can absolutely beat life into shape. As you beat it, you are satisfied. As it changes shape, you are satisfied. When you notice the shape that you beat it into, you are satisfied. Everything becomes a contribution to your state of satisfaction. So, letting life be the way it is doesn't mean not to change it. You will change it totally, but not so that it will get better. You will change it as a game, nothing more. For, you see, if you beat life to change it to be better, that would be coming from dissatisfaction. A lot of people do exactly that. They are not particularly satisfied and their actual impact on the world is even smaller than it seems. Their relationships are relationships of domination and manipulation, the weakest tools of change known on the planet.

NOTE [So, a master practicing starts with the fact that she is whole and complete. Because she says so, and for no other reason. She also starts from the fact that her relationships are whole, complete, and perfect. They are exactly the way they should be. Why? Because she says so, no other reason. As relationships change, that is exactly what they should be doing: changing. When they seem to stay the same, that is exactly what they should be doing: staying the same. When she changes them, that is exactly the appropriate thing to do: change them. When others change them, that is seen as the appropriate thing to happen. How can all this be so? Because our master practicing says so, and for no other reason. This is called living at cause in your relationships.]

I want you to know that in the usual course of events people set out to master their relationships. What I mean by that is not to dominate and manipulate them, except in the highest meaning of those words. However, along the way we invalidate ourselves by causing our relationships to go a certain way without awareness that we cause it. What we say is that it was done to us. This invalidates you and takes your power out of your hands and places it in some other location. You end in confusion. You have to be in confusion and "not know" what happened to avoid awareness of responsibility for what happened. This is not the way of a master practicing in the area of relationship. A master practicing creates the experience of responsibility by intention, even when the understanding of "how" the event was caused has not arrived yet. Understanding comes inevitably. Not the kind of understanding that merely explains things *ex post facto*, but understanding that actually provides mastery of relationships in the present. Understanding like this is best called "knowing." When you know something, confusion has no opportunity to exist. A master practicing in the area of relationships knows, and is willing to know, and everything that happens validates, confirms and contributes to that fact. Because she says so. No other reason.

Chapter Nineteen:
The Result Of Taking A Position

*When you take your position and say it is truth
you are in big trouble.*

I want to hammer a bit on a subject that I have covered elsewhere. I am going to go through it again so that you will become crystal clear on the importance of positionality in your life. As I have said elsewhere, what a mind usually means when it uses the word "truth" is a position that it believes in. The fact is that you exist in a mind while you live on this planet and that is the way it is. <u>Since you exist in a mind, you will always be on a position</u>. Anything you can think of is a position and as soon as you get off that one you are on another one. If you effort and struggle at it you can get on a position called "I am enlightened" or another one called "I am not on a position." Even meditation in its purest form is a position. <u>It is impossible not to have a position.</u>

At the same time you must realize that what you do with your positions is the main source of your karmic suffering in this life. The way that works is that taking a position automatically, mechanically, inevitably, calls into being its opposing position. If I hold up my left arm and say, "Left arm!" I don't have to hold up my right arm and proclaim "Right arm!" Right arm is called into being when I say "Left arm!" If I point to the sky and say "Up!", there is no need to point toward the ground and say "Down!" Down is called into being by "Up!" Likewise, if you take a position about the rightness or wrongness of an issue, that calls into being the opposite, in your own mind, and in the minds of those around you.

So, positions are inevitable and, in and of themselves, are no problem. The problem comes when you assume inappropriate positions and stay on them too long or not long enough. Face it, you can't avoid being on positions. The best you can do is be appropriate about your positions. To be appropriate about your positions you must become extremely conscious of what they are. Most of the world is totally unconscious about the fact that they are sitting on positions. What people say is that their position is truth. When you take your position and say it is truth you are in big trouble. You make the opposing position wrong. The opposing position dwells both in your own mind and in the minds of others around you. Therefore, by sitting on one position as "the truth," you condemn your own mind, as well as the minds of others around you, to be wrong. This results in intense internal turmoil and very dramatic, mechanical relationships. You experience anxiety and emotional ups and downs and your relationships do not work, are not nurturing.

I am not advising you to get off all your positions, since that is impossible. I am advising you to begin to hold your positions as positions and to own the fact that you contain the opposite position at all times, even when you are unconscious of it. When you hold your positions as positions, you have the ability to be appropriate about how long to stay on them and when to get off. If you are willing to acknowledge that you own the opposite positions, you will not have your buttons pushed by others as often. When you react to something someone says in a way that doesn't work, you are always on the position they just espoused and trying to lie about it. I recently had one of my unconscious positions reactivated when a friend of mine stated matter-of-factly that he didn't care if the one billion malnourished people in the world continued to starve or not. Bringing the starvation drama to a close is one of my favorite games in life, so his comment affronted my conscious position and reactivated me against me. What I mean by that is that I also carry the position that I don't care if people starve or not, side by side with the position that I care a lot. Until I processed my anger I was unconscious of the fact that I carried both positions. When you get reactivated or incensed by something someone says to you, the dynamics are always the same.

Creating a context large enough to contain all of your positions, including the ones that you are unconscious about, is what it means to be a big person. When you have such a context, your unconscious positions surface quickly for you to process and you can continue to do what is appropriate to making your life work instead of going off on some nutty tangent. Finally, I want you to know that your positions offered as positions are an absolute contribution. On the other hand, your positions offered as the truth are pure venom.

Chapter Twenty:
The Shift From "I Am" To "I Have"

If you are willing to shift your experience of the content of life from being it to having it, a miracle occurs: you discover that you created all that you have.

The most fundamental error human beings make in life is misidentification of their identity as the "things" in their lives such as clothes, car, house, spouse, body, and any other "things" that one finds in life. The misidentification process begins in the cradle when one notices that there seem to be impulses in the general area. For many years thereafter one thinks something on the order of "I am these impulses" and this gives rise to an irresistible urge to act out the impulses. This brings the child into conflict with others and forces a recognition that he is not impulses but, rather, has impulses. This recognition is absolutely essential to development of the next stage: relationship, the first of which is the relationship with the most nurturing person in the environment. The nurturing received in this relationship is essential to life itself, and the child comes to view himself as "I am this relationship" even before "I am impulse" is fully transformed into "I have impulse." As the relationship matures to separation and individuation the realization comes that one is not relationship and that one *has* relationship. Prior to the transformation from "I am" to "I have" there is a certain selfish quality to the nature of one's relationship with others and to the environment.

The next stage involves family and again the shift is from "I am family" to "I have family" thus accounting for the transformation of attitude toward family as a "thing" to serve one into an entity that presents the opportunity to be of service. An identical process happens with organizations and what I say after this will probably be difficult to fit into your experience. Nevertheless, as we grow older it becomes clear that we are not our bodies and that we do have bodies, that we are not the world and that we do have a world, and that we are not the universe but rather have a universe. One who has expanded from "I am impulse" into the realization that he has a universe is ready to give it up *as an opportunity* and live and die in ecstacy.

Few of us complete the shift from "I am" to "I have" totally and for this reason most of us have the opportunity to begin over and go back for completion. You may very well find yourself shifting back to the beginning, namely "I am impulses" and acting on those impulses, even after you have somewhat mastered some of the latter phases. Don't be perturbed by this for there is no correct order to these lessons. The lesson is of one piece, and it is merely an illusion that it comes in stages. The shift from "I am" to "I have" is the shift from being the content of your life to being the Context of your life; it is about mastery, the kind of mastery which provides complete satisfaction in the face of *any* circumstance; it is the "peace that surpasses understanding" and enables you to make a difference while you live as well as die in complete satisfaction.

Chapter Twenty-One:
Making A Difference

Having your life make a difference is a pure creation which is not dependent on the conditions of your life; nor does it require "proof."

For those who are interested in checking it out, there are several different realities available for experiencing. The reality that you and I are used to I call the "reality of agreement." Within the reality of agreement your individuality does not make a difference. It is supposed to make a difference, people say it makes a difference, but you know deep down that little you doesn't count. You know, for example, that when you go to the polls to vote for a presidential candidate your one measly vote doesn't really count. You have to lie to yourself about it just to con yourself into going to the polls and voting. But you know that little you doesn't make a difference. So, within the reality of agreement, in order to make a difference you have to persuade a number of people to agree with you that you are powerful. This is still how most of the world operates: by domination and manipulation. Some people are very skillful at accumulating a lot of force and using it to their own ends. The only way an individual can count within the reality of agreement is to dominate with force. I say that force is only an illusion of making a difference.

Another reality I choose to call the "drop-out reality." This consists of the use of various chemicals to alter consciousness as well as various techniques of mind/body manipulation which has the effect of placing your consciousness in a place where you really don't count in the world. The whole process is summed up well by the expression "studying your belly-button." Joyful experiences are available in the drop-out reality. If you haven't availed yourself of an experience of this reality, I recommend it to you.

There are many other worthy realities, the religious reality, the scientific reality, to name a few. However, my purpose here is not to catalog the various realities, but simply to remind you that there are different realities. Within all of the various realities that I have so far alluded to, one aspect is held in common: the individual does not make a difference. I am not saying that the individual isn't unique, lovable, special, etc. Individuals can be all of that within the various realities. What I mean is that the individual doesn't really make a difference, doesn't really have a solid, meaningful impact on the quality of life. Most of us know that we don't really make a difference and we live our lives accordingly. You may lie to yourself from time to time, but deep down you know that you don't make a difference. If you are successful at playing in the realities in which you don't make a difference, you can actually become comfortable. You can develop a few special friends, provide for your survival needs comfortably, adopt a special interest in music, literature, etc. You can become snug and secure in a non-pretentious kind of exclusivity. And your life doesn't count. Not really. You never have impact on the world. So, you quit thinking about it. You give up your profound desire to make a real contribution and you settle for being happy. Instead of playing with making a difference in the world, you play with your little problems. Since you are small and your life doesn't make a difference, your special interests and your "problems" make up the grist of your life.

If you don't play successfully in the realities in which you don't make a difference, your problems may get out of hand. As small as they are they will come to look large to miniscule you. You will probably want to talk it out with someone. You may even come to consider yourself as "sick." If you work at it, you can get some agreement that you are "sick." Also, your special interests may get out of hand. You may turn to very unusual interests that will take you out of agreement with the world and cause you problems. All of this can happen only in the realities in which you do not make a difference.

The best you can hope for is a sort of splendid isolation or the accumulation of force, if you are interested in manipulating people. If manipulating people doesn't amuse you, the best you can do is go for splendid isolation. You simply can't hope to make an impact on the world.

On the other hand, there is a reality in which you can *only* make an impact or a difference in the world. That reality is the reality out of which all of the other realities are generated. If you are willing to exist in that reality, your life will make a difference. The reality that generates realities is available only from within you. You can't take a certain chemical or go through a certain mind process or go to a particular church to find this reality. It is available only in your Self.

So, within the Reality of realities everything you do has impact and makes a difference. Of course your mind will want to know "How?" I am sorry, there is no "how." Your making a difference is a pure creation. You simply create it as such. Nor is there "proof" that your life makes a difference. That is, you can't look into your past or review your trophy case to prove that you made a difference. When you exist in the Reality of realities, it isn't important to you to collect proof, trophies, or agreement from others. You simply make a difference, you know it, and you give away the credit to those who need credit. Credit slows you down if what you want to do is make a difference in your lifetime. Credit is something in which you can become stuck.

You will know when you choose to make a difference. You won't need signs. Nevertheless, your mind may want some signs, so let's feed it. First of all you will observe that what you do serves others by your intention; thus serving others is a very prominent characteristic of making a difference. Furthermore, your "problems" will (1) become unimportant and (2) clear up spontaneously. So, not playing in your personal problems is a prominent feature. I am very clear that people create personal problems in their lives because they do not have the experience that their lives matter. When you have the experience that your life matters, personal problems become the transparent illusions that they are. Naturally, you will go out of agreement with the world when you experience that your life makes a difference, but another characteristic of the Reality of realities is that agreement is irrelevant.

Now, I want to tell you the whole truth. You already exist in the Reality of realities. Your life already makes an enormous impact in the world. What you do counts. You may be defending yourself from experiencing the fact that your life makes a difference because (1) you are dependent on agreement or (2) the responsibility of seeing the truth may be too much for you. If you saw the truth that what you do *and don't do* affects the world profoundly, could you continue to live your life the way you are living it now? Be with that question for a moment. Wouldn't you have to make a commitment to be responsible for your impact on the world? Wouldn't you have to absolutely dedicate your life to something and do rather than not do? Wouldn't you have to give up your petty personal problems? I say your life counts. I say that you come from the Reality of realities, the one that created this crummy reality of agreement. Furthermore, I say that deep within you, you know it. You know that what you do, and what you don't do, makes a difference in the world. I say that you can't legitimately deny it and further that, by admitting this to yourself, your life is changed for all time.

Epilogue

In writing these books I have experienced a joy that is beyond description. This has been an opportunity to say to you all of the good things and all of the bad things there were to say, when viewed through the good/bad, right/wrong systems. For now I am complete with you, and these systems are totally transcended. I want you to know that the same things happen in your life when you express yourself totally. What underlies all of the "stuff" you can think of to communicate, all of the ideas you have always wanted to contribute, what underlies your Self, your existence is, "I love you." I love you. And when you know that you love, you can only do what is appropriate to that basic, fundamental experience.

Ron

Invitation

I invite you to correspond with me. You can reach me by writing in care of:

CONTEXT PUBLICATIONS
20 LOMITA AVENUE
SAN FRANCISCO, CALIFORNIA 94122
U.S.A.